The Strange Case of Dr Jekyll and Mr Hyde

ROBERT LOUIS STEVENSON

Level 5

Retold by C. Kingsley Williams and A. G. Eyre
Series Editors: Andy Hopkins and Jocelyn Potter

T0345859

Pearson Education Limited
Edinburgh Gate, Harlow,
Essex CM20 2JE, England
and Associated Companies throughout the world.

ISBN: 978-1-4058-6245-5

First published in the Longman Simplified English Series 1978
First published in the Longman Fiction Series 1993
This adaptation first published by Addison Wesley Longman 1996
First published by Penguin Books 1999
This edition first published 2008

18

Text copyright © Penguin Books Ltd 1999
This edition copyright © Pearson Education Ltd 2008

Typeset by Graphicraft Ltd, Hong Kong
Set in 11/14pt Bembo
Printed in Great Britain by Ashford Colour Press Ltd.
SWTC/07

Cover images: Alamy Images: Chronicle, Kerry Shaw Brown/ Stockimo

Published by Pearson Education Ltd

*Every effort has been made to trace the copyright holders and we apologise in advance for any unintentional omissions.
We would be pleased to insert the appropriate acknowledgement in any subsequent edition of this publication.*

For a complete list of the titles available in the Pearson English Readers series, visit
www.pearsonenglishreaders.com.
Alternatively, write to your local Pearson Education office or to Pearson English Readers
Marketing Department, Pearson Education, Edinburgh Gate, Harlow, Essex CM20 2JE, England.

Contents

Introduction

'I've been learning something about your friend Hyde.'

Dr Jekyll's big healthy face turned pale and an angry look came into his eyes. 'I don't want to hear any more,' said he. 'I thought we'd agreed to drop this matter.'

Dr Henry Jekyll is a well-respected and wealthy doctor in London. He has no family and is looked after by his butler Poole and an army of servants. He does a great deal of good medical work to help patients who are suffering.

Dr Jekyll's two oldest friends are his lawyer, Mr Utterson, and Dr Lanyon. Dr Lanyon, however, has been concerned about the type of scientific work that Dr Jekyll has been doing in the last ten years, which he describes as 'unscientific nonsense'. Mr Utterson is worried when he meets the unpleasant and mysterious Mr Hyde going into Dr Jekyll's house. He discovers that Hyde has great power over Dr Jekyll. A series of nasty events, ending with a murder, appear to be the work of Mr Hyde. Dr Utterson decides to help Dr Jekyll and to try to destroy Mr Hyde. As he does, he learns a horrible secret . . .

Robert Louis Stevenson was born in Edinburgh in 1850. He was an unhealthy child and, like his mother, suffered all his life with breathing problems. He had to spend many hours in bed each winter, while one of the family's servants read to him from the Bible. But when he was well in summer, he showed a wild and carefree nature and loved exploring the countryside. His mother came from a family of lawyers and church ministers and he had a very religious childhood.

His father and grandfather were engineers, and the plan was for Robert to follow in the family tradition. However, he had only studied engineering at Edinburgh University for a short time before he realised that he was no engineer. A sea voyage with his father along the coast showed him the attractions of being an adventurer. He loved the caves and islands and imagined all sorts of stories. To please his family he studied law, but he never worked as a lawyer. He had already decided that he was going to be a writer.

After university, Stevenson travelled in France, meeting and making friends with artists and writers. He met his future wife Fanny Osbourne in Paris. It was love at first sight, but they couldn't marry at once because Fanny was already married. She was living apart from her husband but not yet legally separated. She was ten years older than Stevenson, and an independent 'new woman'. She returned to her native California and in 1879 Stevenson followed her there, travelling and writing across the United States. The journey nearly killed him and Fanny had to nurse him for many months as he recovered.

In 1880, they were finally able to marry. They returned to Britain with Fanny's son, Lloyd, and moved between Scotland, England and France, looking for somewhere that suited Stevenson's health. This was a happy time, when he wrote his most famous works, including *The Strange Case of Dr Jekyll and Mr Hyde*.

After Stevenson's father died in 1887, he took his mother and his family back to the United States. Following his doctor's advice to find a better climate, they then set off for the Pacific Islands and travelled around for three years. In 1890 they settled on the Samoan island of Upolu, where they bought some land and built their own house. Stevenson continued to write and became involved in local politics, criticising the European rulers. He thought they were quite unable to do the job properly. The local people came to him for advice and named him *Tusitala*, Samoan for storyteller.

Stevenson was afraid that he had used up all his creative ideas and he became depressed. He also thought his illness might come back, and he feared that most of all. He said he would prefer 'to be drowned, to be shot, to be thrown from a horse, to be hanged' than to suffer a long, slow illness. He seemed to recover his energy and began writing again. But at dinner one evening he was trying to open a bottle of wine when he suddenly dropped dead. He was forty-four years old.

Stevenson's early writing consisted mainly of short stories and descriptions of his journeys through France. As he travelled across the US from New York to San Francisco in 1789 to find Fanny, he wrote *The Amateur Emigrant*, a well-observed record of American life, including much suffering. His first full-length work of fiction was *Treasure Island*, which came out in 1883. This is the story of Long John Silver and the *Hispaniola*, and has been filmed many times. It brought him fame and success. His fame increased three years later with the very successful *The Strange Case of Dr Jekyll and Mr Hyde* (1886). By the end of the century, more than a quarter of a million copies of the book had been sold. Because of its moral content, it was read by many people who did not usually read novels, and it was referred to in church and religious papers.

Stevenson then wrote three popular Scottish stories, *Kidnapped* (1886), *Catriona* (1893) and *The Master of Ballantrae* (1889). The idea of doubleness, first explored in *The Strange Case of Dr Jekyll and Mr Hyde*, reappears in *The Master of Ballantrae*, where he examines the relationship between two brothers.

While he was in the South Seas, Stevenson wrote two stories about the way the Europeans treated the islands, 'The Beach of Falesa' (1893) and 'The Ebb-Tide' (1894). He was halfway through his last great work, *Weir of Hermiston*, when he died. He is supposed to have said, '[*Weir*] is so good, it frightens me.'

Fanny Osbourne's son, Lloyd, remembers that the idea for *The Strange Case of Dr Jekyll and Mr Hyde* came to Stevenson in a dream. He wrote for three days and nights without stopping. However, Fanny criticised his first attempt, and he burned it and started again. By the end of the week, Lloyd says, he had produced 'sixty-four thousand words in six days'.

Stevenson reached back into his childhood for the idea of Dr Jekyll. There was a famous Scotsman called Deacon Brodie, who was a carpenter by day and a robber by night. As a child, Stevenson had had a chest of drawers made by Brodie in his bedroom in Edinburgh. Perhaps he thought about Brodie during those long periods when he had to stay in bed. Fanny remembered that he had also been very interested in a French scientific paper about levels of consciousness in the human mind. The two ideas gave him the beginning of his story.

There have been many films and plays based on *The Strange Case of Dr Jekyll and Mr Hyde*. None of them stays very close to Stevenson's original story. Most add a romantic interest and do not use the character of Mr Utterson as the main storyteller. Many people think that the best film is still the 1931 Hollywood film, *Dr Jekyll and Mr Hyde*. This starred Fredric March, who won an Oscar for his acting. In the 1971 British film *Dr Jekyll and Sister Hyde*, which connects the story with the famous Jack the Ripper killings in London, Mr Hyde is changed into a woman.

Victoria was queen of Great Britain during Stevenson's lifetime and it was a time of social and industrial change. Scientists and engineers were making new discoveries and inventions all the time, but many people worried that their effect on human beings was often ignored. *The Strange Case of Dr Jekyll and Mr Hyde* presents the view that scientific experiments must be done with the greatest care. It shows how the results can so easily be used for evil instead of good purposes.

Darwin had recently written his *Origin of Species* (1859). The struggle between a person's moral soul and his or low animal nature was widely discussed at the time. Many Victorians believed that only strict moral rules could control the animal desires. Stevenson's Dr Jekyll characterises one of the main problems of the Victorian period. Highly respectable members of society were often guilty of enjoying secret pleasures, involving sex, alcohol and drugs. That is of course true in any age, but Victorian England was organised according to strict moral laws, so it seemed more shocking when those laws were broken. Stevenson never explains exactly what 'pleasures' Jekyll and Hyde are involved in – he leaves the reader to imagine the worst.

The central idea of Stevenson's story has passed into British popular culture. We use the expression 'Jekyll and Hyde' to describe a person with different sides to their personality, one good and one evil. The struggle between the good and evil sides of the same person is the more serious subject of the story, and it is one that Stevenson returns to many times in his work. This may partly be explained by the influence of Stevenson's religious mother. The book uses religious language to describe the fight between Jekyll and Hyde. Stevenson also shows that he is quite sympathetic toward the respectable Dr Jekyll when he is tempted by pleasures of the senses. The same idea of a man without morals is explored by Oscar Wilde in *The Picture of Dorian Gray*, which came out five years after *The Strange Case of Dr Jekyll and Mr Hyde*, in 1891.

Chapter 1 The Story of the Door

Mr Utterson, the lawyer, was a man with a severe expression that was never brightened by a smile. He felt awkward in conversation, and his remarks were short and cold. He rarely showed his feelings. He was tall, thin and dull, but still quite lovable. At friendly meetings, and when the wine was to his taste, a certain human kindness shone in his eye, though it never found its way into his conversation; it showed itself not only in this silent after-dinner look but more often and more loudly in his actions.

He was strict with himself: he drank spirits when he was alone, to destroy his taste for wine, and though he enjoyed the theatre he had not seen a play for twenty years. But he never judged others so strictly; he was sometimes surprised, almost jealous, by the energy shown in their less praiseworthy acts, and he was always readier to help them out of trouble than to blame them. 'I like Cain's remark in the Bible, "Am I my brother's keeper?",' he used to say in his own strange manner of speech. 'I let my brother go to the devil in his own way.' So he was often the last respectable person, and the last good influence, in the lives of men who were on the path to ruin. To such men as these, when they came for his professional advice, he gave the same attention as to anyone else.

No doubt this was easy for Mr Utterson; he was good-natured in everything he did. It is the mark of a man without a high opinion of himself to accept the circle of friends that chance makes for him, and that was the lawyer's way. His friends were men of his own blood, or those whom he had known the longest. No doubt this was the tie between him and Mr Richard Enfield, the well-known man of fashion and his distant cousin. Many people could not understand what these two could see in each other, or what subject they could find in common. It was reported by those who met them on their Sunday walks that they said nothing, looked extremely bored, and would greet with obvious relief the appearance of a friend. But the two men regarded these walks together as the high point of each week, and not only gave up other pleasures but even left the calls of business so that they could enjoy their walks without interruption.

It happened one Sunday that their way led them down a side street in a busy part of London. The street was small and quiet, but on weekdays it did a busy trade. The shopkeepers were all doing well, it seemed, and all hoping to do better still, and they were spending part of their gains on making themselves look more attractive. So the shopfronts stood there with an air of invitation, like rows of smiling saleswomen. Even on Sunday, when it was fairly empty, the street shone out in comparison with its neighbourhood, like a fire in a forest; with its freshly painted woodwork, its well-polished door handles, and its general cleanliness and cheerfulness, it immediately caught and pleased the eye of those who passed that way.

Two doors from one corner, on the left side going east, the line was broken by the entrance to a yard, and just at that point stood a large, ugly building. It showed no windows, nothing but a door on the lower floor and the blind face of a dirty wall on the upper one; its whole appearance bore the marks of long neglect. The door, which was fitted with neither bell nor knocker, had not seen fresh paint for many years. Beggars leaned carelessly against it and struck matches on it; children kept shop on its steps; schoolboys tried their knives on its wooden frame; and for more than twenty years no one had troubled to drive such visitors away or to repair their damage.

Mr Enfield and the lawyer were on the other side of the street. When they came opposite this building, Mr Enfield lifted his stick and pointed.

'Have you ever noticed that door?' he asked, and when his companion agreed that he had he added: 'It's connected in my mind with a very strange story.'

'Really!' said Mr Utterson, with a slight change of voice. 'And what was that?'

'Well, it was like this,' replied Mr Enfield. 'I was coming home from some distant place, at about three o'clock on a black winter morning, and my way lay through a part of London where there was nothing to be seen but lamps. Street after street with all the people asleep, street after street all lit up and all as empty as a church, until at last I got into that state of mind in which a man listens and listens and begins to pray for the sight of a policeman. Suddenly, I saw two figures: a little man who was walking quickly ahead of me, and a girl of eight or ten who was running as hard as she could down a side street. Well, sir, the two ran into each other at the corner, and then came the horrible part of it; the man stepped calmly on the child's body and left her crying with pain and shock on the ground.

'It doesn't sound very serious, but it was terrible to see. He wasn't like a man – he was like some pitiless great machine. I cried out and ran after him and caught him, and I brought him back to the place where there was already quite a group round the unhappy child. He was perfectly relaxed and put up no fight, but he gave me one look, so ugly that it made me tremble. The people who had come out into the street were the girl's own family, and soon the doctor, for whom the little girl had been sent, appeared.

'Well, the child wasn't badly injured; she was more frightened than hurt, according to the doctor. You might have supposed that that would be the end of the matter, but there was one strange thing about it. I had been filled with violent hatred of the man at first sight. So had the child's family, which was only natural. What struck me was his effect on the doctor, who was a very ordinary man, speaking English like a Scotsman and extremely unemotional. Well, sir, he was like the rest of us. Every time he looked at my prisoner, that doctor turned sick and white with the desire to kill him. I knew what was in his mind, just as he knew what was in mine; as killing was impossible, we did the next best thing. We told the man we could and would make such a story of this that his name would fill everyone with disgust from one end of London to the other. If he had any friends or respectability, we promised that he would lose them. And all the time, as we were threatening him, we were doing our best to keep the women off him, because they were as wild as she-devils.

'I'd never seen faces filled with such wild hate. And my man was there in the middle, with a cold scornful look on his face. I could see that he was frightened too; but he spoke to us, sir, like the devil himself.

' "If you choose to take advantage of this accident," said he, "of course I'm helpless. Like any gentleman, I prefer to avoid a scene. Please state your figure."

'Well, we forced him to pay out a hundred pounds to the child's family. He would clearly have liked to refuse. But he could see there was something dangerous in our anger, so at last he agreed. The next thing was to get the money. And where do you think he took us? To that door! He pulled a key out of his pocket, went in, and soon came back with ten pounds in gold and a cheque for the rest. The cheque was payable to "the bearer" at Coutts's Bank, and it was signed with a name that I can't mention, though it's one of the points of my story, a very well-known name. The figure was high, but the signature, if it was real, would have been good enough for much more.

'I pointed out to him that a man doesn't usually walk into a house at four in the morning and come out with another man's cheque for ninety pounds. But he wasn't worried.

' "To set your mind at rest," he said scornfully. "I'll stay with you until the bank opens and present the cheque myself." So we all set off – the doctor, the child's father, this man and myself – and we passed the rest of the night at my house. Next day, after breakfast, we went together to the bank. I handed the cheque in myself, and said I had every reason to believe that the signature was false. But it wasn't. It was perfectly good.'

'Well, well!' said Mr Utterson.

'I see you feel as I do,' said Mr Enfield. 'Yes, it's a nasty story. My man was someone who nobody would want to have dealings with, a really unpleasant man; and the person who wrote the cheque is an extremely respectable gentleman, and (what makes it worse) he is one of those who really does do good in the world. I suppose it's a case of blackmail; an honest man is having to pay heavily for something stupid he did in his youth. But even that, you know, is far from explaining everything.' And with these words he fell into a thoughtful silence.

It was broken by Mr Utterson, asking rather suddenly: 'You don't know whether the man who wrote the cheque lives there?'

'A likely place, isn't it?' replied Mr Enfield. 'But I happen to have noticed his address. It was in some square or other, not in a street.'

'And you never asked about that place with the door?'

'No, sir, I didn't like to,' was the reply. 'I feel very strongly about putting questions. You start one, and it's like starting to roll a stone. You sit quietly on the top of a hill, and away the stone goes, starting others; and soon some kind-looking old man (the last person you would have suspected of any crime) is knocked on the head in his own back garden, and the family have to change their name. No, sir, I make it a rule; the stranger anything looks, the less I ask.'

'A very good rule, too,' said the lawyer.

'But I've studied the place for myself,' continued Mr Enfield. 'It hardly seems like a house. There's no other door, and nobody goes in or out of that one except, very occasionally, the gentleman I met that night. There are three windows on the upper floor, above the yard, though none below; and those windows are always shut, but they're clean. And there's a chimney, which is generally smoking, so somebody must live there. But I'm not quite sure, as the buildings are so packed together that it's hard to say where one ends and another begins.'

They walked on together for some time in silence, until Mr Utterson said: 'Enfield, that's a good rule of yours.'

'Yes, I think it is,' replied Enfield.

'But in spite of that,' continued the lawyer, 'there's one question I want to ask. I want to ask the name of that man who stepped on the child.'

'Well,' said Mr Enfield, 'I can't see what harm it could do if I told you. It was a man called Hyde.'

'Oh,' said Mr Utterson. 'And what did he look like?'

'He isn't easy to describe. There's something wrong with his appearance, something unpleasant, something terrible. He's the nastiest man I ever saw, but I can't really say why. There must be something wrong with the shape of his body, that's what I feel, though I can't explain my feeling. He's a very unusual-looking man, but I can't describe him. And that's not for lack of memory – I can see him clearly in my mind at this moment.'

Mr Utterson again walked some way in silence, and plainly in deep thought.

'You're sure he used a key?' he inquired at last.

'My dear sir . . .' began Mr Enfield, too surprised to say more.

'Yes, I know,' said Mr Utterson. 'My question must seem strange. And if I don't ask you the name of the man who wrote the cheque, it is because I know it already. You see, Richard, your story concerns me closely. If you've been inexact on any point, you'd better correct it.'

'I think you should have warned me,' his cousin replied,

sounding rather offended. 'But I've been perfectly exact. The man had a key, and if you want to know, he still has it. I saw him use it less than a week ago.'

Mr Utterson let out a long breath but said nothing, and Mr Enfield soon went on: 'I've learned another lesson. I shouldn't have spoken. Now I'm ashamed of my overactive tongue. Let's make a promise, never to mention this matter again.'

'With all my heart,' said the lawyer. 'I'll shake hands with you on that, Richard.'

Chapter 2 The Search for Mr Hyde

That evening Mr Utterson came home in low spirits, and sat down to dinner without any desire for food. He had no family, and it was his custom on Sundays, when this meal was over, to sit by the fire with a religious book until the clock on the neighbouring church struck twelve, and then he would go quietly and gratefully to bed. But on this night, as soon as he had finished his dinner, he took a candle and went to his study. There he opened his safe and from a locked drawer in the safe he took out an envelope with 'Dr Jekyll's Will' written on it. Then he sat down with an anxious face to study the document.

It was in Dr Jekyll's own handwriting; Mr Utterson, though he took charge of it when it had been made, had refused to give any help in making it. It said that, in the case of the death of Henry Jekyll, M.D., D.C.L., F.R.S., etc., all his possessions were to pass into the hands of his 'friend Edward Hyde'. But that was not all. In the case of Dr Jekyll's 'disappearance or absence for any period of more than three months', the same Edward Hyde should take his place without delay, just as if he had died, and without any duties except that of paying certain amounts to the people working in the doctor's house. This will had always offended the lawyer's professional feelings. Up to now he had been annoyed because he knew too little of Mr Hyde. Now, by a sudden turn of events, he knew too much. It was bad enough when the name was only a name about which he could learn no more. It was worse when that name began to be clothed with hateful qualities, and, out of the mists that had surrounded it for so long, there suddenly appeared the figure of a devil.

'I thought it was madness,' he said to himself, as he replaced the will in the safe, 'and now I begin to fear that it is shame and dishonour.'

With that he blew out his candle, put on a coat, and set out in the direction of Cavendish Square, where his friend, the great Dr Lanyon, lived.

'Lanyon will know about this, if anyone does,' he thought.

The old butler knew and welcomed him. He was led straight into the dining room, where Dr Lanyon sat alone over his wine. At the sight of Mr Utterson he got up from his chair and welcomed him with both hands. For these two were old friends who had been at school and college together; they not only held each other in great respect but also thoroughly enjoyed each other's company.

After a short discussion of other matters, the lawyer brought up the subject that was troubling him.

'I suppose, Lanyon,' he said, 'you and I must be the oldest friends that Henry Jekyll has?'

'I wish we were younger friends,' Dr Lanyon replied with a laugh. 'But I suppose you're right. Anyway, it makes no difference, I rarely see him these days.'

'Really!' replied Mr Utterson. 'I thought that as doctors you had common interests.'

'We had,' was the reply. 'But it's more than ten years since Henry Jekyll became too fanciful for me. He began to go wrong, wrong in his ideas; and though of course I still take an interest in him because of the past I hardly see him at all. Such unscientific nonsense,' added the doctor, turning suddenly purple with anger at the memory of it, 'would have separated even such friends as David and Jonathan.'

This little show of temper was a relief to Mr Utterson.

'They've only quarrelled on some scientific point,' he thought. 'It's nothing worse than that.' He gave his friend a few seconds to recover and then asked the question that had brought him there.

'Did you ever come across a friend of his, called Hyde?' he asked.

'Hyde?' repeated Dr Lanyon. 'No, I've never heard of him. He must be a new friend.'

That was all the information that the lawyer carried back with him to the great dark bed where he lay restless and awake until daylight came. When the church clock struck six he was still awake, and he had come no nearer to solving his problem.

From then on, Mr Utterson began to watch that door in the side street. Before office hours in the morning, at midday when business was heavy and time was short, at night in the city fog or under the moon, by all lights and at all hours the lawyer was at his chosen post.

And at last his patience was rewarded.

It was a fine dry night, the air was cold, the streets were as clean as a bathroom floor, and the gas lamps, unshaken by any wind, drew a regular pattern of light and shadow. By ten o'clock, when the last shops were closed, the street was silent. Small sounds travelled a long way, and the footsteps of any person coming in his direction reached Mr Utterson's ear long before the person could be seen.

He had been standing there for some minutes when he heard a strange, light footstep coming towards him. In the course of his nightly watches he had grown used to the strange way in which the footsteps of a single person, while he is still a long way off, are suddenly so loud and so clear. But his attention had never before been so sharply attracted. With a mysterious feeling that his efforts were about to succeed, he stepped back into the entrance to the yard.

The steps came rapidly nearer, and grew suddenly even louder as they turned the corner of the street. The lawyer, looking out from the shadows, could see the sort of person that he had to deal with. He was small and very plainly dressed, and the look of him, even at that distance, somehow filled the watching lawyer with disgust. Now the man was crossing the road, towards the door; and as he crossed he pulled a key from his pocket, like someone returning home.

Mr Utterson stepped out into the lamplight and touched him on the shoulder as he passed.

'Mr Hyde, I think?'

Mr Hyde jumped with surprise and breathed in sharply. But his fear passed in a moment and, though he did not look the lawyer in the face, he answered: 'That is my name. What do you want?'

'I see that you're going in,' replied the lawyer. 'I'm an old friend of Dr Jekyll's, Mr Utterson of Gaunt Street. You must have heard my name, and meeting you so conveniently I thought you might let me in.'

'You won't find Dr Jekyll,' replied Mr Hyde. 'He isn't at home.' And then suddenly, but still without looking up, he asked: 'How did you know me?'

'I'll answer that if you'll do something for me,' said Mr Utterson.

'With pleasure. What shall it be?'

'Will you let me see your face?' the lawyer asked.

Mr Hyde seemed to pause, then he suddenly made up his mind and turned confidently towards his questioner. For a few seconds the two men looked closely at each other.

'Now I shall know you when we meet again,' said Mr Utterson. 'It may be useful.'

'Yes,' Mr Hyde agreed, 'it was necessary for us to meet. You'd better have my address as well.' And he gave the number of a house in a street in Soho.

'Good God!' thought Mr Utterson. 'Is he, too, thinking about the will?' But he kept his feelings to himself.

'And now,' said Mr Hyde, 'tell me how you knew me.'

'By description.'

'Whose description?'

'We have common friends,' said Mr Utterson.

'Common friends!' said Mr Hyde. 'And who are they?'

'Jekyll, for example,' said the lawyer.

'He never told you,' cried Mr Hyde, with a burst of anger. 'I didn't think you would lie to me.'

'Come, sir,' said Mr Utterson, 'that is not proper language.'

Mr Hyde gave a scornful laugh, and in the next moment, with unbelievable speed, he had unlocked the door and disappeared into the house.

The lawyer stood where Mr Hyde had left him, looking anxious and confused. Then he went slowly up the street, pausing every step or two to think things through. As Enfield had said, there was something unnatural about the man's body. He had an ugly smile. He had treated the lawyer with a murderous mixture of fear and confidence. He spoke in a strange, rough voice. All these were points against him, but they could not explain the disgust and fear with which Mr Utterson regarded him.

'There must be something else,' he said to himself. 'There *is* something, but I can't find a name for it. God save me, the man seems hardly human! Or is it only an evil soul that poisons and twists his whole appearance? It must be that, I think. Oh, my poor old Harry Jekyll, I've never read the devil's handwriting more clearly on any man's face than on that of your new friend.'

Round the corner there was a square of grand and ancient houses, most of which had lost their honoured place in society and were let as rooms or offices to all sorts of people. But one house, the second from the corner, was still occupied by a single owner and had an appearance of wealth and comfort. It now showed no light except over the front door at which Mr Utterson stopped and knocked. A well-dressed old butler opened the door.

'Is Dr Jekyll at home, Poole?' asked the lawyer.

'I will see, Mr Utterson,' said Poole, admitting the visitor to a large, comfortable hall full of valuable old furniture, which was warmed (as in a gentleman's country house) by a bright wood fire.

'Will you wait here by the fire, sir? Or shall I give you a light in the dining room?'

'Here, thank you,' said the lawyer, and he went to warm himself by the fire.

This hall, in which he was now left alone, was a special fancy of his friend the doctor, and Utterson himself used to speak of it as the pleasantest room in London. But tonight there was a coldness in his blood, the face of Hyde was still fresh in his memory, and he felt (as he rarely did) a sick distaste for life. In these low spirits he seemed to feel a threat of danger in the dancing of the firelight on the polished furniture, and in the shadows that moved restlessly across the ceiling. He was ashamed of his relief when Poole returned to announce that Dr Jekyll had gone out.

'I saw Mr Hyde go in by the old laboratory door, Poole. Is that right, when Dr Jekyll is not at home?' he asked.

'It's quite right, Mr Utterson, sir,' replied the butler. 'Mr Hyde has a key.'

'Your master seems to place a great deal of trust in that gentleman.'

'Yes, sir, he does. We all have orders to obey him.'

'I don't think I've ever met Mr Hyde here, have I?' Utterson asked.

'Oh no, sir. He never eats here,' replied Poole. 'In fact, we rarely see him in this part of the house. He mostly comes and goes by the laboratory door.'

'Well, good night, Poole.'

'Good night, Mr Utterson.'

And the lawyer set out for home with a very heavy heart.

'Poor Harry Jekyll,' he was thinking, 'I'm afraid he's in serious trouble! He was wild when he was young. Of course, that was a long time ago, but in God's law time does not make a person less guilty. Yes, it must be that: some old offence, some hidden shame that is eating away his life like a deadly disease. And punishment has come, slowly but surely, years after memory has forgotten the fault and self-love has excused it.'

Frightened by that thought, he began to worry about his own past, and searched all the corners of his memory for any wrongdoing that might suddenly come to light. His past was fairly blameless; few men could read the record of their lives with less fear. But he was ashamed of the many mistakes he had made and grateful for the memory of other mistakes that he had almost made but had avoided. Then his mind went back to Jekyll's trouble, and a light of hope suddenly shone through the darkness of his thoughts.

'If someone looked into the past of this Mr Hyde,' he said to himself, 'they would surely find that he has secrets of his own. Dark secrets. Secrets that would make poor Jekyll's worst ones seem completely unimportant in comparison. Things cannot continue as they are. It makes my blood go cold to think of this man moving quietly round Harry's house like a thief. And think of the danger of it! If this Hyde knows anything at all about the will, he may grow impatient to get at Harry's money and property. Yes, I must make every effort to destroy this man, if

Harry will let me – if Harry will only let me,' he added, as he saw again in his mind, as clearly as in a mirror, the strange details of his friend's will.

Chapter 3   Dr Jekyll

Two weeks later, by excellent good fortune, the doctor gave one of his pleasantest dinners to five or six old friends, and Mr Utterson managed to remain behind after the others had gone home. This was no new arrangement; it had often happened before. Where Utterson was liked, he was liked very much. Those who invited him loved to keep the serious lawyer a little longer, when their light-hearted and loose-tongued guests were ready to leave. Dr Jekyll always followed this custom. As he now sat on the opposite side of the fire, a large, well-built, smooth-faced man of fifty, sometimes looking a little too clever perhaps, but thoroughly kind and able, you could see by his looks that he was sincerely fond of Mr Utterson.

'I've been wanting to speak to you, Jekyll,' the lawyer began. 'You remember that will of yours?'

Someone watching the doctor closely might have noticed that he found the subject rather unpleasant, but he answered quite cheerfully.

'My poor Utterson,' said he, 'you're unfortunate in having to advise a man like me. I never saw anyone so upset as you were by my will.'

'You know I never approved of it, don't you?'

'Yes, certainly. I know that,' the doctor replied, a little sharply. 'You've told me so several times.'

'Well, I'll tell you so again,' continued the lawyer. 'I've been learning something about your friend Hyde.'

Dr Jekyll's big healthy face turned pale and an angry look

came into his eyes. 'I don't want to hear any more,' said he. 'I thought we'd agreed to drop this matter.'

'What I heard was shameful,' said Utterson.

'It can make no difference. You don't understand my position,' the doctor replied, with a certain confusion of manner. 'I'm in a delicate situation, Utterson, a very strange situation. It's one of those problems that cannot be solved by talking.'

'Jekyll,' said Utterson, 'you know me. I'm a man that you can trust. Tell me what has happened, in confidence. I'm sure I can help you out of your trouble.'

'My dear Utterson,' said the doctor, 'this is extremely kind of you, and I can't find the words to express my thanks. I would trust you more than any man alive, even more than myself, if I could make the choice. But my trouble is not what you imagine; it isn't as bad as that. Just to put your good heart at rest, I'll tell you one thing: I can be rid of Mr Hyde whenever I choose. I promise you that. And I thank you again and again for your concern. But I'll just add one little word, Utterson, and I'm sure you won't be offended. This is a private matter, and I beg you to let it rest.'

Utterson considered this a little, looking into the fire.

'I've no doubt you're perfectly right,' he said at last, getting to his feet.

'Good. But since we've touched on this business, for the last time I hope,' continued the doctor, 'there's one point I should like you to understand. I really have a very great interest in poor Hyde. I know you've seen him; he told me so, and I fear he was rude to you. But I do sincerely take a great interest in him. And if I'm taken away, Utterson, I want you to promise me that you'll be patient with him and get his rights for him. I think you'd do that if you knew everything. It would take a weight off my mind if you would promise.'

'I can't pretend that I shall ever like him,' said the lawyer.

'I don't ask that,' begged Jekyll, laying his hand on his friend's arm, 'I only ask for justice. I only ask you to help him when I'm no longer here.'

Utterson looked at him closely. 'Very well,' he said. 'I promise.'

Chapter 4 The Carew Murder Case

Nearly a year later, one cold October morning, London was shocked by an unusually horrible crime, a crime that attracted particular attention because of the high social position of the victim. The details were few and surprising. A servant girl, living alone in a house not far from the river, had gone upstairs to bed at about eleven o'clock. Although a thick fog rolled over the city before daybreak, the early part of the night had been cloudless, and the narrow street below this girl's window was brightly lit by the full moon. Being a fanciful girl, she sat down by the window and fell into a dream. Never (she used to say, with streaming tears, when she described that experience), never had she felt happier or more at peace. As she sat there, she noticed a pleasant-looking old gentleman with white hair who was coming along the narrow street; and walking towards him there was another gentleman, a very small one, of whom at first she took less notice.

When they met, just below the girl's window, the older man greeted the other very politely. It did not seem as if he had anything very important to say; in fact he appeared from his pointing only to be asking the way somewhere. But the moon shone on his face as he spoke, and the girl was happy to watch it. It showed such old-fashioned kindness, but there was something finer in it too, a sort of confident self-respect.

Then her eye wandered to the other gentleman, and she was surprised to recognize a certain Mr Hyde, who had once visited her employer. On that occasion she had taken an immediate dislike to him. He had in his hand a heavy walking stick, which he was playing with impatiently as he listened to the old man. All of a sudden, without answering, he started shouting in a burst of wild anger, stamping with his foot, wildly waving his stick, and behaving (as the girl described it) like a madman. The old gentleman took a step back, as if he were very much surprised and perhaps rather offended, and at that Mr Hyde completely lost his temper and struck him to the ground. The next moment, he was stamping on him like a wild animal and raining such violent blows on the fallen body that the girl could hear the bones cracking. At the horror of these sights and sounds she then fainted.

It was two o'clock when she recovered consciousness and called the police. The murderer had gone long ago, but there lay his victim in the street, indescribably broken and crushed. The stick which the murderer had used, although it was made of a rare and very hard wood, had been broken in the middle by this mad cruelty; one half lay by the body, the other had doubtless been carried away by the murderer. Some money and a gold watch were found on the victim, but no cards or papers except a sealed and stamped envelope that he had probably been taking to the post. It bore the name and address of Mr Utterson.

This was brought to the lawyer the next morning before he was out of bed. As soon as he saw it and heard about the situation, he looked very worried.

'I shall say nothing until I've seen the body,' he told the policeman. 'This may be very serious. Please wait downstairs while I dress.'

With the same anxious look on his face, he hurried through his breakfast and drove to the police station where the body had been taken.

'Yes,' he said, 'I recognize him. I'm sorry to say that this is Sir Danvers Carew.'

'Good God, sir!' said the police officer. 'Is it possible?' The next moment his eyes lit up with professional interest. 'This affair will cause a great deal of excitement,' he said. 'Perhaps you can help us to find the murderer?' And he described what the girl had seen, and produced the broken stick.

Mr Utterson had already felt anxious at the mention of the name Hyde. When the stick was laid in front of him, he had no more doubts about who had used it, for he recognized it as one that he himself had presented many years before to Henry Jekyll.

'Is this Mr Hyde a short person?' he inquired.

'Particularly small and particularly evil-looking, that's what the girl told us,' said the officer.

Mr Utterson considered this, and then, raising his head, said: 'If you'll come with me in my carriage, I think I can take you to his house.'

As the carriage stopped in front of the Soho address that Hyde had given him, the fog cleared a little and Mr Utterson looked around. He saw a dull and dirty street, a beer shop, a cheap foreign restaurant, a number of poorly clothed children trembling with cold in the doorways, and women of many different nationalities making their way to the shop for a morning glass of beer. The next moment the fog settled down again and cut him off from his evil surroundings. Here was the home of Henry Jekyll's favourite, the man who would be a quarter of a million pounds richer on Jekyll's death.

A silver-haired old woman opened the door. She had an evil face, but her manners were excellent. Yes, she said, this was Mr Hyde's house, but he was not at home. He had come in very late in the night and had gone again in less than an hour; there was nothing strange in that, since his habits were very irregular and he was often away for long periods. Yesterday, for example, was the first time she had seen him for two months.

'Very well then, we wish to see his rooms,' said the lawyer. And when the woman said that it was impossible, he added: 'I'd better tell you who this person is. This is Inspector Newcome, of Scotland Yard.'

A flash of cruel joy appeared on the woman's face.

'Ah!' said she. 'He's in trouble! What has he done?'

Mr Utterson and the inspector exchanged looks.

'He doesn't seem a very popular character,' the policeman remarked. 'And now, my good woman, just let me and this gentleman have a look round.'

In the whole house, which was empty except for the old woman, Mr Hyde had used only two rooms, but these contained expensive furniture and were decorated in good taste. A cupboard was filled with wine, the spoons and forks were of silver, and several good pictures hung on the walls (gifts from Jekyll, Utterson supposed). But at this moment the rooms showed every sign of a recent and hurried search. Clothes lay on the floor, with their pockets inside out, drawers were open, and in the fireplace there was a pile of grey ashes, as if many papers had been burned. From these the inspector picked out the thick end of a green chequebook which had failed to burn. The other half of the broken stick was found behind the door, and as this removed all doubts, the officer said that he was happy. A visit to the bank, where several thousand pounds were found to be lying in the murderer's account, completed his satisfaction.

'I have him in my hands, sir,' he told Mr Utterson. 'You can depend on that. He must have been mad with fear, or he would never have left that broken stick and burned that chequebook. He'll need money, so we have nothing to do but wait for him at the bank, and put out some public notices announcing that he is wanted for murder.'

But describing him in the notices was not so easy. Mr Hyde was known to few; even the girl's employer had only seen him twice. He seemed to have no family, he had never been photographed, and different people gave widely different descriptions, as they usually do. Only on one point did they all agree: there was something mysteriously unnatural about his appearance.

Chapter 5 The Letter

It was late in the afternoon when Mr Utterson reached Dr Jekyll's door, where he was at once admitted by Poole, and led down past the kitchen and across a garden to the building that was known as the laboratory.

It was the first time that the lawyer had been received there, instead of in the house. He examined the dirty, unwelcoming building with interest, and felt strangely uncomfortable as he passed through the silent laboratory itself; chemical equipment covered its tables, open packing cases were scattered around the floor, and a weak light fell through a dusty window high in the roof. At the far end, stairs led up to the doctor's study. This was a large room, lit by three old windows with iron bars that looked out across a yard. Its furniture included a desk, several glass-fronted cupboards, and a long mirror fixed to the wall. A fire was burning and the lamp was already lit on a shelf above it, and there, close to the warmth, sat Dr Jekyll, looking as sick as a man on his deathbed. He did not rise to greet his visitor, but held out a cold hand and welcomed him in a changed voice.

'And now,' said Mr Utterson, as soon as the butler had left them, 'you've heard the news?'

The doctor trembled. 'They were crying it in the square,' he said. 'I heard them from my dining room.'

'One word,' said the lawyer. 'I was Carew's professional adviser, as I am yours, and I want to know what I'm doing. You haven't been mad enough to hide this man?'

'Utterson, I swear to God,' cried the doctor, 'I swear to God I will never see him again. I promise you on my honour that I've finished with him in this world. It's all at an end. In fact, he doesn't want my help. You don't know him as I do. He's safe, quite safe. He'll never be heard of again, you can depend on that.'

The lawyer listened anxiously; he did not like his friend's feverish manner.

'You seem sure of that,' said he, 'and I hope you're right. If he were tried in court, your name might appear.'

'I'm quite sure of it,' Jekyll replied. 'I have reasons to be certain that I can't share with anyone. But there's one thing on which you may advise me. I have − I have received a letter, and I'm wondering whether I should show it to the police. I'd like to leave it in your hands, Utterson. You'll judge wisely, I know.'

'You're afraid, I suppose, that it might lead to his discovery?' asked the lawyer.

'No. I don't really care what happens to Hyde; I've finished with him. I was thinking of my own good name, which this horrible business has rather put in danger.'

Utterson thought for a moment. He was surprised at his friend's words, and yet relieved by them.

'Well,' he said at last, 'let me see the letter.'

The letter was written in an unusual upright hand, and signed, '*Edward Hyde*'. It stated, in very few words, that the writer's friend, Dr Jekyll, whom he had so shamefully treated in return for a thousand kindnesses, need not be worried about his safety, as he had a completely dependable means of escape.

The lawyer was fairly pleased with this letter. It made the friendship seem less shameful than he had thought, and he blamed himself for some of his past suspicions.

'Do you have the envelope?' he asked.

'I burned it,' Jekyll replied, 'before I realized what I was doing. But it had no postmark; it was brought by hand.'

'Shall I keep it and make up my mind in the morning?' Utterson asked.

'I wish you to judge for me,' was the reply. 'I've lost confidence in myself.'

'Well, I shall think about it,' replied the lawyer. 'And now one word more. Was it Hyde who made you put that sentence in your will about "disappearance"?'

The doctor suddenly looked terribly weak; he shut his mouth tightly but his expression made it clear that his friend's guess was correct.

'I knew it,' said Utterson. 'He meant to murder you. You've had a narrow escape.'

'I've had something far more important than that,' replied the doctor. 'I've had a lesson, Utterson. Oh, my God, what a lesson I've had!' And he covered his face for a moment with his hands.

On his way out, the lawyer stopped and had a word or two with Poole. 'A letter came today, by hand,' he said. 'What was the messenger like?'

But Poole was certain that nothing had come except by post. 'And that was only a bill,' he added.

This news brought back all Utterson's fears. Plainly the letter had come through the laboratory door in the side street. Possibly it had even been written in the doctor's study. If that were so, it would have to be differently judged and handled with great care. The newspaper boys, as he went, were crying loudly along the streets: 'Special news! Shocking murder!'

Soon he would be at the funeral of one old friend, and he could not help being rather afraid that the good name of another would be buried in the same grave. It was a very delicate decision that he had to make about the letter, and he began to feel the need for some advice. He could not ask for it directly, but perhaps he could get it in an indirect way.

Half an hour later he was sitting at one side of the fire in his study, with Mr Guest, his head clerk, at the other side. Halfway between them stood a bottle of a particular old wine that he kept for rather special occasions. Outside the windows a cold fog had settled over the city, but inside the room was bright with firelight.

At first he felt awkward, not knowing how to introduce the subject. With the warmth of the fire and the good red wine, this awkwardness gradually melted away. There was no man he trusted more than Guest with professional secrets; in fact, he had sometimes told him more than he meant to. Guest had often been on business to the doctor's house; he knew Poole; he could hardly have failed to hear of Mr Hyde's strange position there; he might already have his own suspicions. Surely, then, he had better see a letter that helped to explain the mystery? Besides, his professional opinion was worth hearing. He would hardly read such a strange letter without making some remarks, and those remarks might guide Mr Utterson's course in dealing with it.

'This is a sad business about Sir Danvers,' he said.

'Yes, sir, it is. It has caused strong public feeling,' Guest replied. 'The man, of course, was mad.'

'I should like to hear your views on that. I've a letter here in his handwriting. It's a secret between ourselves, as I hardly know what to do about it. Whatever it may mean, it's a nasty business. But there it is, and it will interest you: a murderer's handwriting!'

Guest's eyes brightened, and he sat back and studied the letter excitedly.

'No, sir,' he said after a moment. 'The man is not mad, but it's very strange writing.'

'And a very strange writer, by all accounts,' added the lawyer.

Just then a servant entered with a note.

'Is that from Dr Jekyll, sir?' inquired the clerk. 'It is? I thought I recognized the writing. Anything private, Mr Utterson?'

'Only an invitation to dinner. Why? Do you want to see it?'

'For a moment, sir, if I may.' And the clerk laid the two pieces of paper down next to each other and carefully compared them. 'Thank you, sir,' he said at last. 'It's very interesting handwriting.'

There was a pause while Mr Utterson struggled with himself. 'Why did you compare them, Guest?' he asked suddenly.

'Well, sir,' the clerk answered, 'there's a rather strange likeness between them. In many ways they're the same, except for being differently sloped.'

'Rather unusual,' said Utterson.

'It is, as you say, rather unusual,' Guest agreed.

'It would be unwise to speak of this, Guest,' said his employer.

'Yes, sir,' the clerk replied, 'I understand.'

No sooner was Mr Utterson alone that night than he locked the letter signed 'Edward Hyde' in his safe, where it lay from then on. 'What!' he whispered to himself. 'Would Henry Jekyll write a false note and sign it with the name of a murderer?'

Chapter 6 The Mysterious Death of Dr Lanyon

Time passed. Thousands of pounds were offered as a reward for any information, but Mr Hyde had disappeared as if he had never existed. Much of his past was dug up, and it was all shameful. Stories were told of his pitiless cruelty and violence, of his immoral life, of his strange behaviour, of the hatred that seemed to have surrounded him. But not a whisper was heard of his present hiding place. From the time he left the house in Soho on the morning of the murder, he had simply melted into the London fog.

Gradually, as the weeks passed, Mr Utterson began to forget his fears. The death of Sir Danvers was, in his opinion, fully paid for by the disappearance of Hyde. At the same time a new life began for Dr Jekyll, now that Hyde's evil influence had been removed. He went out more frequently, strengthened his ties with old friends, and became once more their familiar guest and entertainer. He had always been known for his generosity to the poor; he was now equally recognized for the strength of his religious beliefs. He was busy; he spent a great deal of time in the open air instead of shutting himself up in his laboratory; he was kind and generous to people, and he did good. The expression on his face was brighter and more sincere, as if with consciousness of service, and for more than two months the doctor was at peace.

On January 8th Utterson had had dinner at the doctor's with a number of others. Lanyon had been there, and their host's eyes had turned from one to the other as in the old days when the three were the closest friends. But on the 12th, and again on the 14th, the lawyer was refused entry to the house.

'Dr Jekyll,' said Poole, 'will go nowhere and see no one.'

On the 15th Utterson tried again, and was again refused. For the last two months he had been seeing his friend almost daily; now he missed his company and felt unhappy without it. The next night he invited Guest to have dinner with him, and the night after that he went to see Dr Lanyon.

There at least he was not refused entry, but when he went in he was shocked at the change that had taken place in the doctor's appearance. He looked like someone who has been threatened with death. His rosy face had grown pale, he had lost a lot of weight and most of his hair, and he looked very much older. But what struck the lawyer was not just these signs of sudden decay in his friend's body; he was struck even more by a look in the eye and a strangeness of manner that could only be caused by some deep-seated terror of the mind. It was unlikely that the doctor would fear death, but that was what Utterson was tempted to suspect.

'Yes,' he thought, 'he's a doctor and he must know his own condition. The knowledge of his coming death is more than he can bear.'

But when Utterson remarked how ill he looked, the doctor declared in a perfectly firm and natural manner that he was a dying man.

'I've had a shock,' he said, 'and I shall never recover. It's a question of weeks. Well, life has been pleasant. I liked it; yes, sir, I used to like it. I sometimes think that if we knew everything, we'd be more pleased to get away.'

'Jekyll's ill, too,' Utterson told him. 'Have you seen him since we had dinner there?'

Lanyon's face changed, and he held up a trembling hand. 'I don't wish to see or hear any more of Henry Jekyll,' he said in a loud, unsteady voice. 'I've quite finished with that person. I beg you to make no further mention of someone who I regard as dead.'

Mr Utterson was shocked by Lanyon's words. Then, after a pause, he asked: 'Can't I do anything? We're three very old friends, Lanyon. We shan't make such friends again.'

'Nothing can be done,' Lanyon replied. 'Ask Jekyll himself.'

'He refuses to see me,' said the lawyer.

'I'm not surprised at that,' was the reply. 'Some day, Utterson, after I'm dead, you may perhaps learn the truth. I cannot tell you. Now, if you can sit and talk with me about other things, stay and do so. But if you can't avoid this unpleasant subject, then in God's name go, because I cannot bear it.'

As soon as he got home, Utterson sat down and wrote to Jekyll, complaining that he was not allowed to see him and asking the cause of his quarrel with Lanyon. The next day brought him a long answer, often very pitifully expressed and sometimes darkly mysterious.

'The quarrel with Lanyon cannot be made to go away,' Jekyll wrote. 'I don't blame our old friend, but I share his view that we must never meet. From now on, I mean to live quite alone. You mustn't be surprised, nor must you doubt my friendship, if my door is often shut even to you. You must let me go my own dark way. I've brought on myself a punishment and a danger that I cannot name. If I have been the most evil of men, I have also suffered the most for my evil. I never imagined that such suffering and terror were possible in this world. There's only one thing that you can do, Utterson, to help me bear what has happened, and that is to ask me nothing about it.'

Utterson could hardly believe what he was reading. Since Hyde's dark influence had been removed, the doctor had returned to his old duties and friendships. A week ago he had been looking forward to a bright and honoured future. But now, in a moment, friendship and peace of mind and the whole course of his life were destroyed. Such a sudden and unexpected change seemed at first like a sign of madness, but when Utterson remembered Lanyon's manner and words, he realized that there must be some deeper cause.

A week afterwards, Dr Lanyon was too ill to leave his bed; and less than two weeks later he was dead. The night after the funeral, at which he had almost cried, Utterson locked the door of his study and, sitting there by the light of one miserable candle, he took an envelope from his pocket. It was sealed with his dead friend's seal and was addressed in the dead man's writing: 'PRIVATE: for G. J. Utterson ALONE, and *to be destroyed unread* if he dies before me.'

The lawyer hardly dared to open it. 'I've buried one friend today,' he thought. 'Supposing this were to cost me another!' Then he felt ashamed of his fear, and broke the seal. Inside, there was another envelope, also sealed, and marked: 'Not to be opened until the death or disappearance of Henry Jekyll.'

Utterson could hardly believe his eyes. Yes, the word was 'disappearance'. Here again, as in the mad will that he had long ago given back to Jekyll, here again was the suggestion that Jekyll might disappear. Written by the hand of Lanyon, what could it mean? His desire to know urged him strongly to ignore Lanyon's wishes and get to the bottom of this mystery; but professional honour and loyalty to his dead friend prevented him, and the envelope was put to rest in the drawer of his private safe.

It is doubtful whether Utterson was so eager, after that day, for the company of his remaining friend. He thought of him kindly, but his thoughts were anxious and fearful. When he went to call, perhaps he was rather relieved to be refused entry. Perhaps, in his heart, he preferred to speak with Poole on the doorstep, surrounded by the fresh air and familiar sounds of the city. Poole had, in fact, no pleasant news to give him. The doctor hardly ever left his study in the laboratory building, and sometimes he even slept there. He was miserable, he had grown very silent, he did not read; it seemed as if he had something on his mind. Utterson became so used to the unchanging nature of these reports that his visits gradually became less frequent.

Chapter 7 The Face at the Window

It happened one Sunday when Mr Utterson was on his usual walk with Mr Enfield, that their way lay once again through the side street, and when they reached the laboratory door, they both stopped to look at it.

'Well,' said Enfield, 'that story's at an end, at least. We shall never see Mr Hyde again.'

'I hope not,' said Utterson. 'Did I ever tell you that I once saw him and shared your feeling of disgust?'

'It was impossible to feel anything else,' Enfield replied. 'But you must have thought me stupid for not knowing that this was a back way into Dr Jekyll's! It was partly your own fault that I ever found that out.'

'So you found it out, did you?' said Utterson. 'In that case, let's step into this yard and take a look at the windows. To tell you the truth, I'm anxious about poor Jekyll; even outside, the presence of a friend might do him good.'

The yard was very cool and rather dark, though the sky, high overhead, was still bright with sunset. The middle one of the three windows was half open; and the person sitting beside it, taking the air with a miserable look on his face like some hopeless prisoner, was Dr Jekyll.

'What! Jekyll!' Utterson cried. 'I hope you're better?'

'I'm in a very poor state,' replied the doctor in a tired voice. 'But it won't last long, I thank God for that.'

'You stay inside too much,' said the lawyer. 'You should be outside, taking exercise, like Mr Enfield and me. Let me introduce you: my cousin Mr Enfield, Dr Jekyll. Come now. Get your hat, and take a quick walk with us.'

'You're very kind, and I'd like to very much,' the doctor sighed. 'But, no, no, no, it's quite impossible. I don't dare to. But I'm very glad to see you, Utterson; this is really a great pleasure. I'd ask you and Mr Enfield to come in, if this place were fit for guests. I'm afraid it isn't.'

'Why then,' said the lawyer good-naturedly, 'the best thing we can do is to stay out here, and speak with you from where we are.'

'That's just what I was going to suggest,' the doctor replied, with a smile. But the words were hardly spoken when the smile was suddenly struck from his face, and it was followed by an expression of complete terror and uncontrollable misery that froze the blood of the two gentlemen below the window. They only saw it for a moment, as the window was immediately closed; but that moment had been enough, and they turned and left the yard without a word. In silence, too, they walked along until they turned the corner into the next street, where even on a Sunday there were people about. Then Mr Utterson stopped and looked at his companion. They were both pale, and each saw his own horror in the other's eyes.

'God forgive us! God forgive us!' said Mr Utterson.

The two men walked on once more in silence.

Chapter 8 Dr Jekyll's Last Night

Mr Utterson was sitting by his fireside one evening after dinner when he was surprised to receive a visit from Poole.

'Good heavens, Poole, what brings you here?' he cried. Then, taking a second look, he added: 'What's the matter? Is the doctor ill?'

'Mr Utterson,' said the butler, 'there's something wrong.'

'Take a seat, and here's a glass of wine for you,' the lawyer answered kindly. 'Now, there's no hurry; just tell me plainly what you want.'

'You know the doctor's ways, sir,' Poole began. 'You know how he shuts himself up. Well, he's shut up again in his study, and I don't like it, sir, I swear I don't like it. Mr Utterson, sir, I'm afraid.'

'Now, my good man,' said the lawyer, 'tell me plainly. What are you afraid of?'

'I've been afraid for about a week,' the butler told him, without answering the question, 'and I can't bear it any longer.'

The man's appearance proved the truth of his words. His manner was unusually nervous, and except when he first announced his fear he had not looked the lawyer in the face. Even now, he sat with the glass of wine untasted in his hand, and with his eyes directed to a corner of the floor. 'I can't bear it any longer,' he repeated.

'Come,' said the lawyer, 'I see you have some good reason to be afraid, Poole. I see there's something seriously wrong. Try to tell me what it is.'

'I think there's been a horrible crime,' said Poole in a broken voice.

'A horrible crime!' cried the lawyer, a good deal frightened, and rather angry with himself because of that. 'What horrible crime? What do you mean?'

'I daren't say what I mean, sir,' was the answer. 'But will you come along with me and see for yourself?'

Mr Utterson's only reply was to rise and get his hat and coat. But he noticed with wonder the look of relief on the butler's face and, with no less wonder, the fact that the wine was still untasted when Poole put down his glass.

It was a wild, cold night with a pale moon, which was lying on its back as if the wind had blown it over. It certainly seemed to have swept everyone off the streets; Mr Utterson had never known them to be so empty, just when he would rather have seen them crowded. In spite of all his efforts to remain calm, his mind was filled with fear that some terrible thing was about to happen.

The square, when they got there, was full of wind and dust. Poole, who had kept a few steps ahead, now stopped outside the house, and in spite of the freezing weather he took off his hat and wiped his hot face. But it was hot from fear, not from violent exercise; his face was white, and when he spoke his voice was weak and nervous.

'Well, sir,' he said, 'here we are, and I pray that my fears have been mistaken.'

'So do I, Poole,' said the lawyer.

The butler knocked gently on the door, and a voice inside asked: 'Is that you, Poole?'

'Yes, it's all right,' said Poole. 'Open the door.'

The hall, when they entered it, was brightly lit. All the servants, men and women, were crowded together there like frightened sheep. At the sight of Mr Utterson, the servant girl burst into a flood of tears, and the cook, crying out, 'Thank God! It's Mr Utterson,' ran forward as if to throw her arms around him.

'What, what? Are you all here?' said the lawyer, in annoyance. 'Very irregular, very improper. Your master would be far from pleased.'

'They're all afraid,' said Poole.

Silence followed. It was an admission of their fear. Then the cook gave a wild cry and started crying again. Poole told her to be quiet, in an angry voice that showed the state of his own nerves, because when the woman had cried out they had all turned suddenly towards the inner door with frightened faces.

'And now,' continued the butler, addressing the kitchen boy, 'bring me a candle, and we'll get this done immediately.' Then he begged Mr Utterson to follow him, and led the way to the back garden.

'Now, sir,' said he, 'come as quietly as you can. I want you to hear, and I don't want you to be heard. And see here, sir, if by any chance he asks you in, don't go.'

Mr Utterson's nerves, at this unexpected ending, gave a jump that nearly threw him off balance; but he recovered his courage and followed the butler into the laboratory building and up to the foot of the stairs. Here Poole signalled to him to stand on one side and listen, while he himself, putting down the candle, went slowly up the steps and knocked with a rather uncertain hand on the study door.

'Mr Utterson, sir, asking to see you,' he called, and once more he signalled violently to the lawyer to listen.

A voice answered from inside. 'Tell him I can't see anyone,' it said complainingly.

'Thank you, sir,' said Poole, with a note of satisfaction in his voice. Taking up his candle, he led Mr Utterson back across the garden and into the great kitchen, where the fire was out and mice were running across the floor.

'Sir,' he said, looking Mr Utterson in the eyes, 'was that my master's voice?'

'It seems much changed,' replied the lawyer, very pale, but returning the look.

'Changed? Well, yes, I think it is,' said the butler. 'When I've been twenty years in this man's house, could I be deceived about his voice? No, sir. My master's been got rid of. He was got rid of eight days ago, when we heard him cry out in the name of God.

'And who's in there instead of him, and why it stays there, is a question that cries to heaven for an answer, Mr Utterson!'

'This is a very strange story, Poole. This is rather a wild story, my man,' said Mr Utterson, biting his finger. 'Suppose it were as you suggest. Supposing Dr Jekyll to have been, well, murdered. What could persuade the murderer to stay? That doesn't make sense, it isn't reasonable.'

'Well, Mr Utterson, you're a hard man to satisfy, but I'll do it,' said Poole. 'All this last week he, or it, or whatever lives in that study, has been crying night and day for some sort of medicine, and cannot get what he wants. It was sometimes his custom, my master's that is, to write his orders on a sheet of paper and throw it on the stairs. We've had nothing else this week: nothing but papers on the stairs, and a closed door, and even his meals have had to be left there for him to take in when no one was looking. Well, sir, every day, and two or three times a day, there have been orders and complaints, and I've been rushing off to all the chemists in London. Every time I brought the order back, there would be a note telling me to return it because it wasn't pure, and then another order to a different chemist. Whatever this drug's for, sir, it's wanted terribly urgently.'

'Do you have any of these papers?' asked Mr Utterson.

Poole felt in his pocket and brought out a note, which the lawyer, bending nearer to the candle, carefully examined. It said: 'Dr Jekyll thanks Maw & Co. for their attention. He is sorry to inform them that the drug they sent him is impure and quite useless for his present purpose. Two years ago, Dr J. bought quite a large quantity of it from Maw & Co. He now begs them to search with the greatest care, and if any of the same quality is left, to send it to him now, whatever it costs. The importance of this to Dr J. cannot be overstated.' So far the letter had run quietly, but here, with sudden wild movements from the pen, the writer's feelings had broken loose. 'In God's name,' he had added, 'find me some of the old medicine.'

'This is a strange note,' said Mr Utterson. Then he added sharply: 'Why is the envelope open?'

'The man at Maw's was very angry, sir, and he threw it back to me as if it was dirt,' Poole replied.

'This is unquestionably the doctor's writing, isn't it?' asked the lawyer.

'I thought it looked like it,' said the butler, rather bitterly. Then, in a different voice: 'It doesn't matter what the writing's like,' he said. 'I've seen him!'

'Seen him?' repeated Mr Utterson. 'Well?'

'It was like this,' said Poole. 'I came suddenly into the laboratory from the garden. It seems that he had slipped out to look for this drug. The study door was open, and there he was, at the far end of the room, digging among the boxes. He looked up when I came in, gave a kind of cry, and rushed upstairs into the study. I only saw him for a minute, but the hair stood up on my head. Sir, if that was my master, why did he have a mask on his face? If it was my master, why did he cry out and run from me? I've served him long enough to be trusted. And then . . .' he paused, and passed his hand over his face.

'This is all very strange,' said Mr Utterson, 'but I think I begin to see daylight. Your master, Poole, has plainly caught one of those diseases that both give the sufferer terrible pain and slowly destroy his whole body. That explains it all: the change in his voice, his wearing a mask and avoiding his friends, and his eagerness to find this drug by means of which the poor man still hopes to recover his health. I pray God that he may not be disappointed! There's my explanation. It's a sad one, Poole, and terrible to consider; but it's plain and natural and makes good sense, and delivers us from all fanciful fears.'

'Sir,' said the butler, turning paler, 'that thing wasn't my master, and there's the truth. My master,' here he looked round him, and began to whisper, 'is a tall, well-built man, and this thing was quite short.'

Utterson attempted to interrupt. 'Oh, sir,' cried Poole, 'do you think I don't know my master after twenty years? Do you think I don't know where his head reaches to in the study doorway, where I saw him every morning of my life here? No, sir, that thing in the mask was never Dr Jekyll; God knows what it was, but it was never Dr Jekyll. It's the belief of my heart that he has been murdered.'

'Poole,' replied the lawyer, 'if you say that, it will become my duty to make certain. Although I have no desire to upset your master, and although this note to the chemist seems to prove him to be still alive, I shall consider it my duty to break in that door.'

'Ah, Mr Utterson, now you're talking!' cried the butler.

'And here comes the second question,' Utterson continued. 'Who's going to do it?'

'Why, you and I, sir,' was the reply.

'That is very well said,' the lawyer told him, 'and whatever happens, I shall take care that you are not blamed.'

'There's an axe in the laboratory,' said Poole, 'and you might take this iron bar for yourself.'

The lawyer picked up the iron bar and balanced it in his hand.

'Do you know, Poole,' he said, looking up, 'that you and I are about to place ourselves in a position of some danger?"

'You may say so, sir.'

'Then we'd better be honest with each other,' said the lawyer. 'We both think more than we've said. Now let's say just what we think. This masked figure that you saw, did you recognize it?'

'Well, sir, it went so quickly, and its body was so strangely bent, that I could hardly swear to anything,' the butler answered. 'But if you mean "Was it Mr Hyde?", why, yes, I think it was! You see, it was roughly his size, and it had the same quick light way of moving, and who else could have got in by the laboratory door? You've not forgotten, sir, that at the time of the murder he still had the key with him. But that's not all. I don't know, Mr Utterson, if you ever met this Mr Hyde?'

'Yes,' said the lawyer, 'I once spoke with him.'

'Then you must know, as well as the rest of us do, that there was something strange about that gentleman, something that made you feel quite ill with shock. I don't really know how to describe it, sir, beyond this: it was something you felt in your bones, something cold and thin.'

'I admit I felt something of what you describe,' said Mr Utterson.

'Quite so, sir,' replied Poole. 'Well, when that masked thing like a monkey jumped from among the chemicals and rushed into the study, it went down my backbone like ice. Oh, I know it isn't proof, Mr Utterson; I'm educated enough for that. But a man has his feelings, and I give you my word on the Bible that it was Mr Hyde.'

'Yes, yes,' said the lawyer. 'My feelings tend the same way. Evil, I fear, brought him and your master together, and evil was sure to come of such a connection. Yes, truly, I believe you. I believe poor Harry is killed, and I believe his murderer (for what purpose, God alone can tell) is still hiding in his room. Well, we must catch him. Call Bradshaw.'

The servant answered Poole's call, looking very pale and frightened.

'Calm yourself, Bradshaw,' said the lawyer. 'This fearful uncertainty has been bad for the nerves of all of you, I know; but we now intend to put an end to it. Poole and I are going to force our way into the study. If all is well in there, I'm quite ready to bear the blame. But in case anything is really wrong, or in case any criminal tries to escape, you and the boy must go round the corner with a pair of good sticks, and take your post at the laboratory door. We give you ten minutes to be ready at your places.'

As Bradshaw left, the lawyer looked at his watch. 'And now, Poole, let's get to ours,' he said. And taking the iron bar under his arm, he led the way through the garden into the laboratory, where they sat down silently to wait. The faint sounds of London went on all around; but nearer at hand the stillness was broken only by the sound of footsteps going up and down the study floor.

'It walks like that all day, sir,' whispered Poole, 'and for the greater part of the night as well. Only when a fresh drug comes from the chemist is there any break. Ah, sir, there's the blood of a murdered man in every step! But listen again, a little closer. Put your heart in your ears, Mr Utterson, and tell me if that's the doctor's footstep.'

The steps fell lightly and strangely, with a certain swing, although they went so slowly; they were very different from the heavy noisy footsteps of Henry Jekyll. Utterson sighed. 'Is there never anything else?' he asked.

'Once,' Poole answered, 'once I heard it crying!'

'Crying? What kind of crying?' asked the lawyer, conscious of a sudden icy feeling of horror.

'Crying like a woman or a lost soul,' said the butler. 'I came away so upset that I too could have cried.'

But now the ten minutes had come to an end. Poole pulled out the axe from under a packing case; the candle was placed on the nearest table to provide light for their attack; and, hardly breathing, they went slowly towards the room where that patient foot was still walking up and down, up and down, in the quiet of the night.

'Jekyll,' cried Utterson, in a loud voice, 'I demand to see you.' He paused a moment, but there was no reply. 'I give you fair warning, we think there's something wrong, and I must and shall see you,' he went on; 'if not by fair means, then by unfair ones. If not by your invitation, then by force!'

'Utterson,' said the voice, 'in God's name, don't come in!'

'Ah, that's not Jekyll's voice, it's Hyde's!' cried Utterson. 'Break the door down, Poole!'

Poole swung the axe over his shoulder; the blow shook the building, and the door jumped against the lock. A terrible cry, as of pure animal terror, rang through the study. Up went the axe again, and again the door jumped. Four times the blow fell, but the wood was hard and the fittings were excellently made, and it was not until the fifth blow that the lock burst apart, and the wreck of the door fell inwards on the floor.

The attackers, horror-struck by their own violence and by the stillness that followed it, stood back a little and looked into the room. There it lay in the quiet lamplight, a good fire burning cheerfully with water heating over it, a drawer or two lying open, papers neatly set out on the desk and, nearer the fire, the things arranged for tea; the quietest room in London that night, you would have said, and, except for the glass-fronted cupboards full of chemicals, the most ordinary one.

Right in the middle there lay the body of a man, horribly twisted and not yet quite still. They went towards it carefully, turned it on its back, and recognized the face of Edward Hyde. He was dressed in clothes that were far too big for him, clothes of the doctor's size. The muscles of his face still moved as if he were alive, but life was quite gone; and by the broken bottle in the hand and the strong smell that hung in the air, Utterson knew that he was looking at the body of a self-destroyer.

'We have come too late,' he said sadly, 'either to save or to punish. Hyde has paid for his crimes with his own life. It only remains for us to find the body of your master.'

They now thoroughly examined the whole building. Besides the laboratory and the study there were only storerooms and a few big dark cupboards. Each needed only a quick look, for they were all empty, and the dust that fell from their doors showed that all had long remained unopened. Nowhere was there any sign of Henry Jekyll, dead or alive.

Poole stamped on the floor of the passage.

'He must be buried here,' he said, listening to the sound.

'Or he may have run away,' said Utterson, and he turned to examine the door into the side street. It was locked, and a rusty key was lying near it on the floor.

'This doesn't look as if it has been used for a long time,' the lawyer remarked.

'Used!' cried Poole. 'Don't you see, sir? It's broken, just as if a man had stamped on it.'

'Ah,' said Utterson, 'and the broken edges are rusty too.' The two men looked at each other, wondering what this meant. 'This is beyond me, Poole,' the lawyer continued. 'Let's go back to the study.'

They went up the stairs in silence, and with an occasional frightened look at the dead body they examined everything in the room, even more thoroughly than before. At one table there were signs of chemical work with various measured piles of some white salt on some small glass plates, as if the unhappy man had been interrupted during some experiment.

'That's the same drug that I was always bringing him,' said Poole. And as he spoke, the water heating above the fire suddenly boiled over.

This brought them to the fireside, where the chair was drawn up and the tea things stood beside it, even with sugar in the cup. There were several books on a shelf, and one lay open beside the tea things. Utterson was surprised to see that it was a religious work which Jekyll had several times urged him to read, and that some surprisingly irreligious notes had been written on it in the doctor's own writing.

Next, the searchers came to the long mirror and looked into its depths with nervous fear. But it showed them nothing except the firelight shining endlessly from the glass-fronted cupboards, and their own pale and frightened faces looking in.

'This mirror has seen some strange things, sir,' whispered Poole.

'And surely none was stranger than itself,' replied the lawyer, also in a whisper. 'What did Jekyll . . .' he paused, half afraid to ask himself the question, 'what could Jekyll want it for?'

'I have no idea,' said Poole.

Next they turned to the desk. Among the neat piles of papers there was an envelope on which was written, in the doctor's writing, the name of Mr Utterson. The lawyer opened it, and several papers fell to the floor. The first was a will, as strangely worded as the one he had returned to the doctor six months before; but in place of the name of Edward Hyde, the lawyer read, with indescribable surprise, the name of Gabriel John Utterson. He looked at Poole, and then back at the will, and last of all at the dead man stretched on the floor.

'I don't understand,' he said. 'He has been here for days. He had no cause to like me. He must have been angry to see my name instead of his. But he has not destroyed this paper.'

He picked up the next one. It was a short note in the doctor's writing, and dated at the top.

'Oh, Poole!' the lawyer cried. 'He was alive and here today. His body can't have been removed in such a short time. He must still be alive, he must have run away! But then, why would he run away? And how? And if he did, can we safely say that this man killed himself? Oh, we must be careful. I've a feeling that we may still cause your master to suffer some terrible end.'

'Why don't you read that note, sir?' asked Poole.

'Because I'm afraid to,' replied the lawyer. 'I pray God that I may find no cause for my fears!' And with that he fixed his eyes on the paper and read as follows:

My dear Utterson,

When this comes into your hands, I shall have disappeared. I cannot be certain as to how that will happen, but my feelings and all the suspicions of my situation tell me that the end is sure and must come soon. Go then, and first read the story which, Lanyon warned me, he was going to place in your hands; and if you wish to hear more, turn to the story of,

Your ashamed and unhappy friend,

HENRY JEKYLL.

'There was a third paper?' asked Utterson.

'Here, sir.' said Poole, and handed to him a fat envelope that was sealed in several places.

The lawyer put it in his pocket.

'We'd better say nothing about this. If your master has run away or is dead, we may at least save his good name. It's now ten o'clock. I must go home and read these papers in quiet; but I shall be back before midnight, when we shall send for the police.'

They went out, locking the door of the laboratory behind them. And Utterson, leaving the servants once more round the fire in the hall, walked slowly back to his own study to read the two stories in which this mystery was now to be explained.

Chapter 9 Dr Lanyon's Story

On January 9th, now four days ago, I received by the evening post an envelope addressed in the handwriting of my colleague and old schoolfriend, Henry Jekyll. I was a good deal surprised by this, for we were by no means in the habit of writing to each other. I had seen the man, and had dinner with him, the night before, and I could imagine no reason why he should send me a letter. The subject of it increased my wonder, for this is how the letter ran:

10th December

Dear Lanyon,

You are one of my oldest friends, and although we may have disagreed at times on scientific questions, I cannot remember any break in our friendship. There was never a day when, if you had said to me, 'Jekyll, my life, my honour, my balance of mind, all depend on you,' I would not have given my fortune or my left hand to help you. Lanyon, my life, my honour, my balance of mind are all in your hands; if you fail me tonight, I am lost.

I want you to delay all other plans for tonight, yes, even if you were called to the bedside of a queen; I want you to hire a carriage and, with this letter in your hand, to drive straight to my house. Poole, my butler, has his orders; you will find him waiting for you with a locksmith. The door of my study is then to be forced open. You are to go in alone: to open the glass door of the cupboard (marked with an E) on the left side, breaking the lock if necessary; and to take out, with *everything* in it, the fourth drawer from the top or (which is the same thing) the third from the bottom. In my extreme state of mind, I have a terrible fear of misdirecting you. You will know the right drawer by what it contains: some powders, a small glass bottle, and a notebook. I beg you to carry this drawer back with you to Cavendish Square.

That is the first part of my request; now comes the second. You should be back, if you set out as soon as you receive this, long before midnight. At midnight, then, I have to ask you to be alone in your study, to admit with your own hand into the house a man who will present himself in my name, and to place in his hands the drawer that you will have brought from my study. Then you will have played your part and earned my undying thanks. Five minutes afterwards, if you demand an explanation, you will have understood that these arrangements are of the greatest possible importance, and that by failing to do any one of them, regardless of how strange it seems, you might have caused my death or the loss of my mind.

Though I am confident that you will treat this despairing request with all seriousness, my heart sinks and my hand trembles at the possibility of your failing me. Think of me at this hour, in a strange place, in darker hopelessness than the wildest fancy could describe, but knowing that, if you will help me, my troubles will roll away like a story that is told. Help me, my dear Lanyon, and save,

Your friend,

H. J.

P. S. I had already sealed this when a fresh terror struck my soul. It is possible that the post office may fail me, and that this letter may not come into your hands until tomorrow morning. In that case, dear Lanyon, do what I have asked when it shall be most convenient for you in the course of the day, and once more expect my messenger at midnight. It may then already be too late; and if that night passes without event, you will know that you will never see Henry Jekyll again.

On reading this letter, I was sure my friend was mad. But until that was proved beyond the possibility of doubt, I felt I had to do as he requested. The less I understood of this wild story, the less I could judge its importance; and a request made in such words could not lightly be ignored. So I left my dinner table, called a carriage, and drove straight to Jekyll's house. The butler was expecting me; he had received by the same post as mine a letter containing his orders, and had sent immediately for a locksmith and a carpenter. These men came while we were still speaking, and we moved together to the laboratory. The door of the study was very strong, and its lock was excellent; the carpenter thought he would have great trouble, and would have to do a lot of damage, if force were used; and the locksmith was near despair. But he was a skilful man, and after two hours' work the door stood open. The cupboard marked E was unlocked; and I took out the drawer, had it packed up and tied in a sheet, and returned with it to my house.

Here I examined what it contained. The powders were quite carefully packed, but not with the neatness of a chemist; so it was plain that Jekyll had made them up himself, and when I opened one of the wrappers I found something that seemed to be a simple white salt. The bottle, to which I next turned my attention, was perhaps about half full of a blood-red liquid. The book was an ordinary notebook and contained little but a list of dates. These covered a period of many years, but I noticed that they had stopped quite suddenly a year ago. Here and there a short remark was added to a date, usually no more than a single word: 'double' appeared perhaps six times in a total of several hundred notes; and once, very early in the list, 'total failure!!!'.

All this, though it sharpened my interest, told me little. How could the presence of these things in my house affect either the honour, the mind or the life of my fanciful friend? If this messenger could come to one place, why could he not go to another? And why was this gentleman to be received by me in secret? The more I thought about it, the more certain I grew that I was dealing with a case of brain disease. Though I sent my servants to bed, I loaded an old gun, so that I would be ready to defend myself.

Twelve o'clock had hardly rung out over London when the knocker sounded very gently on the front door. I opened it myself and found a small man leaning miserably against the doorpost.

'Have you come from Dr Jekyll?' I asked.

He quickly answered, 'Yes', and when I requested him to enter, he did so with a searching backward look into the darkness of the square. There was a policeman not far off, with a lamp in his hand, and at the sight of him my visitor seemed to come inside with increased urgency.

These details made me anxious, and as I followed him into the bright light of my study, I kept my hand ready on my weapon. Here, at last, I had a chance to see him clearly. I had never seen him before, that was quite certain. He was small, as I have said. I also noticed the shocking expression on his face, the muscular activity of his otherwise weak body, and, last but not least, the unpleasant effect that his closeness had on my feelings.

This person was dressed in a fashion that would have made an ordinary person laughable; his clothes, although they were of fine material, were far too large for him in every measurement. The trousers hung away from his legs and were rolled up to keep them off the ground; the waist of the coat came below his stomach, and the collar was spread wide across his shoulders. For some strange reason this laughable appearance was far from moving me to laughter. To my interest in his nature and character, there was added a desire to know something of his origin, his life, his fortune and position in the world.

These thoughts, though they have taken so much space in writing, were the work only of a few seconds. My visitor was on fire with excitement.

'Have you got it?' he cried. 'Have you got it?' And his

impatience was so great that he even laid a hand on my arm and tried to shake me.

I was conscious, as he touched me, of a certain icy pain running through my blood. I pushed him away.

'Come, sir,' said I. 'You forget that I have not yet the pleasure of knowing you. Be seated, if you please.' And I set him an example, sitting down in my usual seat and with as much of my ordinary professional manner as the late hour, the nature of my thoughts, and my horror of my visitor, would let me show.

'I beg your pardon, Dr Lanyon,' he replied, quite politely. 'What you say is perfectly true; my impatience has made me forget my manners. I come here at the request of your friend, Dr Henry Jekyll, on business of great importance, and I understood . . .' he paused and put a hand to his throat, and I could see, in spite of his calm manner, that he was struggling against some uncontrollable feelings, 'I understood that a drawer . . .'

But here I took pity on my visitor's anxiety, and also perhaps on my own growing desire for an explanation.

'There it is, sir,' said I, pointing to the drawer, which lay on the floor behind a table and was still covered with a sheet.

He rushed to it, and then paused and laid his hand on his heart. I could hear his teeth moving against each other, and his face was so pale and so full of horror that I grew extremely worried.

'Calm yourself,' I said.

He gave me a horrible smile and then, as if with the decision of despair, he pulled away the sheet. When he saw what was under it, he gave one loud cry of such relief that I sat there speechless. And the next moment, in a voice that was already fairly well under control, 'Have you a glass measure?' he asked.

I rose from my place with quite an effort, and gave him what he asked. He thanked me with a smile, measured out a few drops of the red liquid and added one of the powders. The mixture, which was at first a dark red, soon began to brighten in colour and to give off a little gas. Suddenly, and at the same moment, the mixture changed to a dark purple, and then more slowly to a watery green. My visitor, who had watched this with an eager eye, smiled, put the glass down on the table, and then turned and examined my face.

'And now,' he said, 'let's settle what is to be done. Will you be wise? Will you be guided? Will you let me take this glass in my hand and leave your house without further talk? Or has your desire to know too strong a hold on you? Think before you answer; it shall be done as you decide. If you wish, you shall be left as you were before, neither richer nor wiser, unless the sense of service done to a man in terrible pain may be counted as riches of the soul. Or, if you prefer it, new knowledge and new roads to fame and power shall be opened to you, here in this room, immediately; and your eyes will be blinded with wonder at a sight that would frighten the devil himself.'

'Sir,' said I, pretending to be much calmer than I really was, 'you speak mysteriously, and you will perhaps not be surprised if I hardly believe you. But I have gone too far in the way of strange services to pause now before I see the end.'

'Very well,' replied my visitor. 'Lanyon, remember your professional honour; what follows must be a secret between us, as doctors. And now, you who have so long held the most narrow and traditional views, you who have scorned the idea that medicine can go beyond the laws of nature, you who have laughed at wiser men, watch this!'

He put the glass to his lips and drank. A cry followed. He lost his balance and half fell, then caught at the table and held on, his eyes red and wild, breathing heavily. And as I watched there came, I thought, a change; he seemed to swell, his face became suddenly black, and its shape seemed to melt and rearrange itself, and the next moment I had jumped to my feet and back against the wall, with my arm raised to hide me from that unnatural sight and with my mind full of terror.

'Oh, God!' I cried, and 'Oh, God!' again and again. For there in front of my eyes, pale and suffering from shock, and half fainting, and feeling blindly around him with his hands, like a dead man who has come back to life, there stood Henry Jekyll!

My mind is too confused to write down what he told me in the next hour. I saw what I saw, I heard what I heard, and it made my soul sick. But now, when that sight has disappeared from my eyes, I ask myself if I believe it, and I cannot answer. My life is shaken to its roots; sleep has left me, and terror sits by me at all hours of the day and night. I feel that my last day is coming, and that I must die; but still I shall die in disbelief. As for the evil that that man has made known to me, I cannot think of it without a shocked feeling of horror, even though I cry with shame at the memory of it. I will tell you only one thing, Utterson, and that (if you can force your mind to believe it) will be more than enough. The person who came to my house that night was, by Jekyll's own admission, known by the name of Hyde and hunted for in every corner of the land as the murderer of Carew.

HASTIE LANYON

Chapter 10 Henry Jekyll's Full Statement of the Case

I was born into a rich family and was also gifted with excellent abilities, I had a natural taste for hard work, and I valued the respect of the wise and the good among those around me; so I was certain, you might have thought, to become a respected and honourable man.

The worst of my faults was a kind of impatient excitement and desire for entertainment, such as has made many men happy; but I found it hard to combine this with my strong desire to carry my head high and to wear a serious expression in public. So I kept my pleasures secret; and when I grew old enough to think deeply and to consider my progress and position in the world, I found myself already living a double life.

Many men would even have spoken proudly of such wrongdoings as I was guilty of; but from the high standard that I had openly set for myself, I regarded them with a deep sense of shame. Though I led this double life, both sides of my character were completely sincere. I was no more myself when I allowed my self-control to slide and sank into secret shame, than when I publicly directed all my efforts to scientific studies and to the relief of suffering.

I had reached this stage when my laboratory experiments began to throw light on the matter. I began to realize, more deeply than anyone has yet stated, how changeable and how insubstantial this solid-looking body is in which we walk. I found that certain drugs have the power to shake and pull apart our covering of flesh, just as the wind might blow a curtain to one side. At last I even managed to mix a drug that would change the whole substance of my body and mind, and would reshape them in a new way that would be no less natural because it was the clear expression of the lowest qualities in my soul.

I waited for a long time before I tested this idea experimentally. I knew well that I risked death; any drug that so powerfully controlled my inner nature might, if I took too much of it, completely destroy the body that I wanted it to change. But the thought of such a powerful discovery at last made me overcome my fears. I had already prepared the liquid; I now bought a large quantity of a particular salt from a chemist, which I knew, from my experiments, to be the one thing still needed, and late one night I mixed the drugs. I watched them boil and steam in a glass, and, with a burst of courage, I swallowed the mixture.

The most terrible pains followed: I experienced aching bones, violent sickness, and a sense of horror that cannot be worse at the hour of birth or death. Then these pains quickly began to pass, and I recovered as if I had been suffering from a serious illness. I felt something strange in my blood, something indescribably new, unbelievably sweet. I felt younger, lighter and happier in body; in my mind, I was conscious of a wild current of disordered fancies and of an unknown and slightly evil freedom of the soul. I knew, at the first breath of this new life, that I was the slave of my original evil, but much worse, ten times worse; and the thought of this strengthened and pleased me like wine. I stretched out my hands, taking pleasure in the freshness of these feelings, and as I did I suddenly realized that I had lost height.

There was no mirror in my study at that time. Filled with hope and with the pride of success, I decided to go out in my new shape as far as my bedroom. I crossed the yard; I walked softly along the passages, a stranger in my own house; and when I arrived at my room I saw for the first time the appearance of Edward Hyde.

I spent only a moment in front of the mirror. The second and decisive experiment had still to be attempted. It remained to be seen whether I had lost myself beyond recovery and must escape before daylight from a house that was no longer mine. Hurrying back to my study, I prepared and drank the mixture once more; once more I suffered the pains of death, and once more I recovered, but with the character and the appearance of Henry Jekyll.

That night I had come to a deadly crossroads. If I had considered my discovery in a better frame of mind, if I had carried out the experiment while under the influence of good intentions, everything would have been different; from these pains of death and birth I would have come out as a servant of God and not of the devil. The drug itself was neither bad nor good. It simply shook the doors of the prison of my character, and the evil spirits that had been locked there were suddenly freed. At that time all goodness in me was asleep; my evil was ready to seize its opportunity, and the thing that it produced was Edward Hyde. So although I now had two characters as well as two appearances, one was completely evil; the other was still the old Henry Jekyll, that strange mixture of whose improvement I had already learned to despair. So the tendency was completely towards the worse.

Even at that time I had not yet gained control of my distaste for a life of study. I still liked to have a good time. And as my pleasures were, to say the least, unsuited to a respectable doctor, and I was not only well known but also growing rather old, this struggle between my two characters was daily becoming more unwelcome.

My new power tempted me until I fell and became its slave. Simply drinking the mixture, I could be free of the body of the doctor and wear instead, like a mask, that of Edward Hyde. I smiled at the idea, which seemed to me at the time to be amusing, and I made my preparations with particular care.

First I took that house in Soho to which Hyde was tracked by the police; and I employed as housekeeper a person who, I well knew, possessed a silent tongue and no particular respect for the law. Then I announced to my servants that a Mr Hyde, whom I described, was to be freely accepted in my house in the square and that they were to do as he asked; and I even called and made myself known to them in my second character. I next prepared that will, to which you, Utterson, so strongly objected, so that if anything happened to me while I was Henry Jekyll, I could continue in the person of Edward Hyde without loss of my possessions. When I had made all the arrangements I could to protect my interests, I began to make use of the strange freedom of my position.

Men have, before now, hired others to do their crimes for them. I was the first that ever did so just for pleasure. I was the first who could appear respectable in the eyes of the public, but could in a moment, like a schoolboy, throw off the clothes of respectability and jump head first into the sea of freedom. In my unrecognizable mask, I was completely safe. Think of it, I did not even exist! Just let me escape into my laboratory, just give me a second or two to mix and swallow the drugs that were always ready, and Edward Hyde, whatever he had done, would disappear like a breath on a mirror. And there instead, quietly at home, working late at night in his study, would be Henry Jekyll, a man who could afford to laugh at any suspicion.

I do not intend to describe in detail the wrongs that I allowed my other self to do (even now I can hardly believe that I did them). I mean only to point out the warnings with which my punishment gradually arrived. There was an accident, which I just mention, as no serious trouble followed; an act of cruelty to a child stirred the anger of a witness, whom I recognized a few days ago as your cousin. A doctor and the child's family joined him. There were moments when my life was in danger. Finally, in order to satisfy them, Edward Hyde had to bring them to my door and pay them with a cheque signed by Henry Jekyll. But this danger was easily avoided for the future by opening an account at another bank in the name of Edward Hyde himself; and when, by sloping my writing backwards, I had supplied him with a signature, I thought I would be safe.

Some two months before the murder of Sir Danvers, I had been out for one of my adventures, had returned at a late hour, and woke in the morning with a rather strange feeling. I looked around me, saw the familiar furniture of my big bedroom, and recognized the pattern of the curtains round my bed. In spite of all this, something still kept telling me that I was not where I was, that I had not woken where I seemed to be, but in the little room in Soho where I used to sleep in the body of Edward Hyde.

I smiled to myself, and lazily wondered why I felt so strange, but I was still half asleep and my eyes kept closing. I was still in this dreamy state when, opening my eyes for a moment, I noticed my hand. Now, the hand of Henry Jekyll (as you have often remarked, Utterson) was large, firm, white and well made, a good doctor's hand. But the hand which I now saw lying on the bedclothes, in the misty yellow light of a London morning, was thin and bony, with rough dark skin, and covered with thick black hair. It was the hand of Edward Hyde.

I must have looked at it for half a minute in stupid wonder before terror woke in my heart, as sudden and frightening as a crash of thunder. I jumped from my bed and rushed to the mirror. At the sight that met my eyes, my blood ran cold. Yes, I had gone to bed as Henry Jekyll, and I had woken as Edward Hyde!

How was this to be explained? And, here came another rush of terror, how was it to be put right? It was morning, and the servants were up. All my drugs were in the study, a long journey (down two flights of stairs, along a passage, across the garden and through the laboratory) from the place where I was then standing, horror-struck. Perhaps it might be possible to cover my face. But what was the use of that, when I was unable to hide my change in size?

And then, with a powerful feeling of sweet relief, I remembered that the servants were already used to the coming and going of my second self. I had soon dressed, as well as I could, in clothes of my own size. I walked through the house, where the servants stood back on seeing Mr Hyde at such an hour and so strangely clothed. And ten minutes later, Dr Jekyll had returned to his own shape and was sitting down, with an anxious face, trying to eat his breakfast.

Certainly I had no desire for food. This strange event, so unlike my earlier experiences, seemed to be spelling out the letters of my future. I began to consider, more seriously than ever before, the possible effects of my double existence. My evil half had recently been well exercised and fed. It seemed as if the body of Edward Hyde had grown larger: as if, when I wore that form, I were a stronger man. I began to recognize a danger that the balance of my nature might be changed, and that the character of Edward Hyde might become mine for ever. The power of the drug had not been always equal. Once it had completely failed me. Since then I had been forced on more than one occasion to double the mixture; and once, at risk of death, I had had to take three times the usual amount. These had been the only dark moments, so far, in my new life. But now, in the light of that morning's experience, I realized that, although my original problem had been to escape from the body of Jekyll, the opposite situation had gradually but decidedly come into effect. Everything, therefore, seemed to point to this: I was slowly losing hold of my original and better self, and slowly becoming my second and worse self.

I now felt I had to choose between these two. My two natures had memory in common but all other powers were most unequally shared between them. Jekyll shared in the pleasures and adventures of Hyde; but Hyde cared nothing for Jekyll, or remembered him only as the robber remembers the hole in the mountain where he hides. If I chose to be Jekyll, I would lose forever those pleasures to which I had given way in secret and had now begun to give way more frequently. If I chose to be Hyde, I would lose a thousand interests and hopes; I would become, immediately and for ever, scorned and friendless. The choice might appear clear, but there were other considerations.

Though Jekyll would suffer bitterly in the struggle for self-control, Hyde would not even know what he had lost. My own situation was strange, of course, but this struggle is as old and as ordinary as man. And so, as you would expect, I chose the better part and then found that I had not the strength to keep it.

Yes, I preferred the middle-aged and dissatisfied doctor, surrounded by friends and full of honest hopes; and I said goodbye to the freedom, the light step, the excitement and the secret pleasures that I had enjoyed in the younger character of Hyde. My choice was made perhaps with some unconscious doubts, for I neither gave up the house in Soho nor destroyed the clothes of Edward Hyde, which still lay ready in my study. But for two months I was true to my determination. For two months I led a purer life than I had ever managed before.

But time began at last to dull the freshness of my fear. I began to suffer the pains of strong desire, as if Hyde were struggling for his freedom. And at last, in a moment of moral weakness, I once again mixed and swallowed the magic drink.

My devil had been long caged. He came out with a wildness you cannot imagine. I was conscious, even when I took the drug, of a more uncontrolled and more desperate desire for evil. It must have been this, I suppose, that stirred in my soul that storm of impatience with which I listened to the polite words of Sir Danvers Carew. No man in his right mind could have been guilty of that crime. But I had consciously destroyed the balance that gives even the worst men a degree of steadiness when faced with temptation; if I were tempted, however slightly, I was certain to fall.

Immediately the spirit of the devil woke in me and ran wild. With evil joy I hammered his old body and took real pleasure in every blow. Only when my arm grew tired was I suddenly, in the middle of my mad anger, struck through the heart by a cold terror. I saw that my life was in danger, and I rushed from the scene. But my heart was as full of excitement as of fear, and my desire for evil was both encouraged and increased. I ran to the house in Soho and, to hide my tracks, I destroyed my papers. Then I hurried home through the lamplit streets.

Hyde had a song on his lips as he mixed the drugs, and as he drank he gave a cheer for the dead man. The pains had not finished tearing him when Henry Jekyll, with streaming tears of relief and guilt, fell on his knees and raised his hands to God in prayer. I could have cried out loud. I tried with tears and prayers to drown the horrible sights and sounds that crowded through my memory. Even while I prayed, the ugly face of my evil side looked deep into my soul. But this guilty despair was followed by a sense of joy, because the problem of my double life was solved. Hyde was now impossible. I locked the door in the side street, through which he had so often passed, and stamped on the key until it broke!

The next day there came the news that the murder had been seen, that Hyde's guilt was clear to the whole world, and that the murdered man was an honoured public figure. It was not only a crime, it was a senseless act. But I think I was glad to have my better nature guarded now by the terror of being hanged. Jekyll had become my hiding place. If Hyde were to show his face for a moment, the hands of all men would be raised against him to take him to his death.

I was determined that my future way of life should prove my sorrow for the past. I can honestly say that this determination did produce some good. You know how seriously I worked to relieve suffering during the last months of last year. You know that I did much for others, and that the days passed quietly, almost happily, for myself. I cannot truly say that I grew tired of this useful life; in fact, I think I enjoyed it more fully every day. But my double nature was still with me; and as time dulled the sharpness of my sorrow, the lower side of me, which I had given way to for so long and had so recently chained down, began demanding to be let loose. Not that I dreamed of bringing Hyde back to life; even the idea of that would frighten me to madness. No, it was in my own person, as Henry Jekyll, that I was once more tempted to give way to temptation.

There comes an end to all things. The deepest measure is filled at last, and this giving way to my evil desires destroyed the balance of my soul. But I was not afraid. The fall seemed natural, like a return to the old days before I had made my discovery. It was a fine clear day, and Regent's Park was sweet with the smells and sounds of spring. I sat in the sun on a garden seat. The animal side of my nature was still tasting the memory of its pleasures; the spiritual side was a little sleepy, promising to show sorrow later but not yet ready to begin. After all, I thought, I was like my neighbours.

Then I smiled, comparing myself with other men, comparing my active goodness with the lazy cruelty of their neglect. And at the moment of that proud thought a horrible sickness seized me, with terrible trembling. This passed away, and left me faint. Then, as in its turn the faintness also passed, I began to feel a greater confidence, a scorn of danger, a loosening of the ties of duty. I looked down. My clothes hung shapelessly on my shortened body, and the hand that lay on my knee was bony and hairy. I was once more Edward Hyde!

A moment earlier I had been wealthy and respected, even loved, with the table set for me in the dining room at home. Now everyone was on my track; I was hunted, homeless, a known murderer, with a sure end on a hangman's rope.

My courage was shaken, but it did not fail me completely. I have more than once noticed that, in my second character, my mind seemed sharpened to a point and I could recover quickly from any shock. So, in a situation where Jekyll would have sunk in despair, Hyde rose to the importance of the moment. My drugs were in one of the cupboards in my study. How was I to reach them? That was the problem that, pressing my hands against my head, I set myself to solve. I had no key to the laboratory door in the side street. If I tried to enter by the front door of the house, my own servants would seize me. I saw that I had to employ another hand and I thought of Lanyon. But how could I reach him, and persuade him? Even supposing that I escaped recognition in the streets, how was I to make my way into his presence? And how could I, an unknown and unpleasant visitor, persuade the famous doctor to break into another doctor's study? Then I remembered that one part of my original character remained unchanged: I could write in Jekyll's handwriting. As soon as this idea came to me, the way that I had to follow became clear.

I arranged my clothes as neatly as I could, hired a carriage, and drove to a hotel in Portland Street whose name I remembered by chance. The driver could not hide his amusement at my appearance. I looked at him with an expression of devilish anger, and the smile froze on his face, luckily for him, and even more luckily for myself; if it had not, I would certainly have dragged him off his seat.

As I entered the hotel, I looked around with such an angry face that the people working there trembled. They did not dare exchange looks in my presence. They took my orders, led me to a room, and brought me a pen and paper. Hyde in danger of his life was a new person: shaking with violent anger, ready for murder, eager to cause pain. But he was clever. He controlled his anger with a great effort, and wrote his two important letters, one to Lanyon and one to Poole.

After that, he sat all day by the fire in his private room, biting his nails. There he took his dinner, alone with his fears, while the waiter clearly trembled at his look. And from there, when night had fallen, he set out in a closed carriage and was driven up and down the streets of the city. 'He' I say, I cannot say 'I'. That child of the devil had nothing human about him; nothing lived in him except fear and hatred. And when at last, thinking that the driver had begun to distrust him, he dismissed the carriage and continued on foot (a noticeable object in his badly fitting clothes), the violence of that fear and hatred exploded inside him like a storm. He walked fast, hunted by his fears, talking wildly to himself, hiding in the shadows of the loneliest streets, and counting the minutes that still separated him from midnight. Once a woman spoke to him, offering, I think, a box of matches. He struck her in the face, and she ran away.

When I recovered myself at Lanyon's, my old friend's horror may have had some effect on me. I do not know. It was in any case only a drop in the ocean, compared with the sick hatred with which I looked back on these hours. A change had come over me. It was no longer the fear of the hangman; it was the horror of being Hyde that I suffered from. Partly in a dream I listened to Lanyon's cries of terror and anger against me; and partly in a dream I came home to my house and went to bed. I slept so heavily that even the terror of my dreams could not wake me until morning. Then I woke, feeling shaken and weakened but refreshed. I still hated and feared the thought of the devil that slept inside me, and I had not of course forgotten the terrible dangers of the day before; but I was once more at home, in my own house and close to my drugs, and thanks to God for my escape filled my soul with a new hope.

I was stepping across the yard after breakfast, breathing the cool morning air with pleasure, when I was seized again by those indescribable feelings that were the first sign of the change. I only just had time to gain the shelter of my study before I was once more burning and freezing with the violent desires of Hyde. On this occasion it took a double amount of the mixture to bring me back to my proper self. And six hours later, as I sat looking sadly at the fire, the pains returned and the drug had to be taken again.

In short, from that day on it was only by a great effort, and only under the immediate action of the drug, that I was able to wear the face of Jekyll. At all hours of the day and night I was seized by the sudden trembling; above all, if I slept for a moment in my chair, even lightly, I always woke as Hyde.

I was now so worn out by this continuous danger, and by the sleeplessness that it forced on me, that I became seriously weak and feverish both in body and mind. And my mind was occupied by one thought alone: the horror of my other self. But when I slept, or when the effect of the drugs wore off, I passed almost in a moment (for day by day the pains grew less) into the possession of a soul boiling with hatred for everything, and a body that did not seem strong enough to hold the explosive energy of its desires.

It is useless to say more, and I have no time. No one has ever suffered in such a terrible way – let that be enough. But my punishment might have gone on for years if I had not had this last misfortune, which now separates me for ever from my own face and nature as Henry Jekyll. My original supply of powdered salt, which had lasted since I first began to use it, began to run low. I sent out for a fresh supply, and mixed the drug. The colour changed once, but not a second time. I drank it, and it had no effect. You will learn from Poole how I have had London searched, from end to end, without success. I now have to accept the fact that the first supply was impure, and that this unknown impurity gave the drug its special power.

About a week has passed, and I am now finishing this statement under the influence of the last of the old powders. This, then, is the last time, unless heaven takes pity on me, that Henry Jekyll can think his own thoughts or see his own face (how sadly changed!) in the mirror. And I must not delay too long before bringing my writing to an end; if my story has so far escaped destruction, it has been by a combination of great care and good luck. If the pains take me in the act of writing this, Hyde will tear it to pieces; but if enough time has passed after I have written, it may be saved once again from his scorn.

The end that is closing round us both has already changed and crushed him. Half an hour from now, I know how Hyde will sit shaking and crying in my chair, or march restlessly up and down this room (his last hiding place on earth) listening in terror for any sound of possible danger. Will Hyde be hanged on the public hangman's rope? Or will he find the courage to take his own life at the last moment? God knows. I do not care. This is my true hour of death, and what follows concerns a person who is not myself. Here, then, as I lay down the pen and seal up my last words, I bring the life of that unhappy Henry Jekyll to an end.

ACTIVITIES

Chapter 1

Before you read

1 Do you know the story of Dr Jekyll and Mr Hyde? What do you think the relationship is between them?

2 Read the Introduction to this book and answer these questions.
  a Where does the story take place?
  b How does Dr Lanyon describe Dr Jekyll's work?
  c Why doesn't Dr Utterson like Mr Hyde?

3 Match these words from the story with their meanings. Then check your answers in the Word List at the back of the book.
  axe blackmail butler candle experiment mask muscle victim

  a something to hide your face   e a light
  b a part of your body   f a crime
  c a way to make discoveries   g a male servant
  d a person who suffers a crime   h a tool

4 Look again at the Word List at the back of the book. Complete this paragraph with words from the list.

  My .... and I arrived at the house early. We could see immediately that it was .... and unloved. There were bits of .... old metal lying around outside. When the owner arrived, we felt .... because we didn't even want to go inside. We were not .... to buy it and we felt a sense of .... when we got back into our car and drove away.

While you read

5 Circle three words or phrases that describe Mr Utterson.
  a man of fashion kind chatty bad-tempered serious
  good-natured unkind cheerful

6 Circle the correct answers.

   a On their walk, Mr Enfield and Mr Utterson stop in a street where the shops are all *well-kept/closed*.

   b Mr Enfield tells *a nasty/an amusing* story.

   c A man and a girl *ran into/met* each other; the man *stepped on/helped* the girl.

   d The girl's family, the doctor and Mr Enfield all wanted to *kill/ignore* the man.

   e The man *agreed/refused* to pay money to the girl's family.

   f Mr Utterson *knows/doesn't know* the man who lives in the white house, *but it isn't/and it is* Hyde.

After you read

   7 No one can describe Mr Hyde properly. Why do you think this is? What do you think he looks like?

   8 Describe the building in which Hyde seems to live. What makes the men think that he lives there?

Chapter 2

Before you read

   9 Discuss these questions.

   a Who lives in the white house and whose name is on the cheque?

   b Mr Utterson would like to forget Mr Enfield's story and continue with his normal life. Do you think he will? Why (not)?

   c Mr Utterson thinks that Hyde is blackmailing the man who lives in the white house. Do you agree?

While you read

10 Answer *Yes* or *No* to these questions.

   a Is Mr Utterson married?   .....

   b Is he Dr Jekyll's lawyer?   .....

   c Does he approve of Dr Jekyll's will?   .....

   d Does the will come into effect only if Dr Jekyll dies?   .....

   e Have Mr Utterson and Dr Lanyon known each other long?   .....

   f Has Dr Lanyon met Mr Hyde?   .....

11 Choose the correct answers.

    a How does Mr Utterson feel about Dr Jekyll's situation after his meeting with Mr Hyde?

      worse   better

    b What does Mr Hyde think of Mr Utterson, do you think?

      an old fool   a frightening enemy

    c What is Mr Utterson's impression of Mr Hyde?

      a devil   a strange, rough character

    d How does Mr Utterson get into Dr Jekyll's house?

      through the laboratory door   through the front door

    e Who knows about Mr Hyde in Dr Jekyll's house?

      all the servants   only Poole

After you read

12 Work with a partner and have this conversation.

    Student A: You are Mr Utterson. After your visit to Dr Jekyll's house, imagine that you go back to see Dr Lanyon. Discuss what power Mr Hyde may have over Dr Jekyll. Why does he allow him to move around his house like a thief? Why has he left him all his money?

    Student B: You are Dr Lanyon. Ask your friend about his visit to Dr Jekyll's house. Discuss the questions that are worrying him.

Chapters 3–4

Before you read

13 Mr Utterson decides to try and destroy Hyde at the end of Chapter 2. What will he do, do you think?

14 We meet Dr Jekyll in the next chapter. What do you expect him to be like? Talk to a partner.

While you read

15 Are these sentences true (✓) or false (✗)? Correct the false ones.

    a Dr Jekyll is pleased to talk about the will.   .....

    b The doctor is able to tell Mr Utterson about his trouble.   .....

    c He says it is as bad as Mr Utterson imagines.   .....

    d He explains that he can get rid of Mr Hyde whenever
       he wants.   .....

    e Mr Utterson says that he will like Mr Hyde more as
       he knows him.   .....

    f After the conversation Mr Utterson feels more
       sympathetic to Mr Hyde.   .....

16 Complete this newspaper report of the Carew murder. Use these
words:

attack   fainted   directions   stolen   eleven o'clock   two o'clock
walking stick   witness   moon   murdered   bones

DANVERS CAREW MURDER SHOCKS LONDON

At .... last night, under a bright full ....,
Sir Danvers Carew was .... Sir Danvers did nothing
more than ask for .... when a strange man, known as
Mr Hyde of Soho, started to .... him. Hyde beat Sir
Danvers with a .... and stamped on him until all his
.... were broken and he was dead. A ....
in a house near the scene .... at this point and did
not wake until .... Sir Davers' money and gold watch
were not ....

17 Who or what is

    a dull and dirty?   ....

    b silver-haired?   ....

    c decorated in good taste?   ....

    d half-burned?   ....

    e behind the door?   ....

After you read

18 Work in pairs and have this conversation.

    Student A: You are a newspaper reporter. Ask Inspector Newcome for details of the murder.

    Student B: You are Inspector Newcome. Answer the reporter's questions.

Chapter 5

Before you read

19 Discuss these questions.

    a Where do you think Mr Hyde is hiding?

    b Will the police find him?

While you read

20 What two things make Utterson suspicious in this chapter? Complete these sentences.

    a Poole tells Utterson that no letters ....

    ....

    b Hyde's handwriting is ....

    ....

After you read

21 How has Dr Jekyll changed when Mr Utterson visits him at home?

Chapters 6–7

Before you read

22 Will Dr Jekyll's life improve now that Hyde has disappeared?

23 Who do you think will say or write these things to Mr Utterson?

    a 'I've had a shock and I shall never recover.'

    b 'If I have been the most evil of men, I have also suffered the most for my evil.'

    c 'Well, that story's at an end at least. We shall never see Mr Hyde again.'

24 Number these events in the correct order from 1 to 7.

    a Dr Lanyon dies. .....

    b Mr Hyde disappears completely. .....

    c Dr Jekyll suddenly refuses to go out or see anyone. .....

    d Dr Jekyll, Dr Lanyon and Mr Utterson meet together
       as old friends. .....

    e Mr Enfield and Mr Utterson see Dr Jekyll at his window. .....

    f The two men watch in horror as Jekyll's face changes. .....

    g Mr Utterson puts Dr Lanyon's letter unopened in his safe. .....

After you read

25 If you were Mr Utterson and you had Dr Lanyon's letter in your hand, would you open it or put it in your safe?

26 Describe what you think Mr Utterson and Mr Enfield see.

Chapter 8

Before you read

27 The next chapter is called 'Dr Jekyll's Last Night'. What do you think is going to happen?

While you read

28 Are these sentences right (✓) or wrong (✗)?

    a Poole visits Mr Utterson. .....

    b The streets are full of people. .....

    c Dr Jekyll's servants are all in the kitchen. .....

    d Poole has collected orders from chemists all
       over London. .....

    e Poole breaks down the door with an axe. .....

    f Hyde is dead. .....

    g Hyde has shot himself. .....

After you read

29 Answer the questions.

    a What increases Mr Utterson's fear on the way to Dr Jekyll's house?

    b Who has seen Dr Jekyll in the last week?

    c Before they break down the door, what do Poole and Mr Utterson think has happened to Dr Jekyll?

    d What is the person in the room doing while Poole and Mr Utterson are breaking down the door?

    e Why do you think Dr Jekyll had a long mirror in his room?

30 Work with two other students and have this conversation. Mr Utterson has gone home and you are in the kitchen.

    Students A and B: You are Bradshaw and the cook. Ask Poole what happened in the laboratory.

    Student C: Answer Bradshaw and the cook's questions.

Chapter 9

Before you read

31 Discuss these questions.

    a What was the terrible shock that killed Dr Lanyon?

    b Where is Dr Jekyll now?

While you read

32 Complete these sentences.

    a Dr Lanyon receives a .... from Dr Jekyll.

    b Dr Jekyll asks Dr Lanyon to fetch a .... of powders and liquids from his study.

    c At midnight there is a .... at Dr Lanyon's door.

    d A horrible, small man comes in and mixes a bottle of ....

    e He drinks it and suddenly the small man .... and changes into Dr Jekyll.

    f Dr Jekyll tells him that the small man was ....

33 What emotions does Dr Lanyon experience when he sees Hyde change into Dr Jekyll?

34 Discuss these questions.

    a Henry Jekyll writes to Dr Lanyon and asks him to fetch drugs from his study. Why doesn't Jekyll get the drugs himself?

    b Dr Lanyon cannot remember what Dr Jekyll told him about his experiments. Why not, do you think?

Chapter 10

Before you read

35 These sentences come from Dr Jekyll's letter to Mr Utterson. What is Dr Jekyll writing about, do you think?

    a 'I experienced aching bones, violent sickness and a sense of horror that cannot be worse at the hour of birth or death.'

    b 'With evil joy I hammered his old body and took real pleasure in every blow.'

    c 'I have had London searched, from end to end, without success.'

While you read

36 Are these sentences right (✓) or wrong (✗)?

    a Dr Jekyll began his double life when he first took his new drug.   .....

    b He hated the feeling of pure evil that controlled his body after he swallowed the drug.   .....

    c The character of Hyde gradually became weaker than the character of Jekyll.   .....

    d After Hyde killed Carew, Dr Jekyll decided never to bring Hyde back to life.   .....

    e A few months later, Dr Jekyll went out and enjoyed the pleasures of the night.   .....

    f He became Hyde again but he couldn't get to his drugs.   .....

    g He hoped that Hyde would have the courage to kill himself before he was captured.   .....

After you read

37 Why are these important in Henry Jekyll's Statement?
powdered salt   a rusty key   handwriting

38 Discuss these questions.
  a Why was Dr Jekyll tempted to experiment with the drug?
  b If you take away a sense of shame and responsibility from a human, will the evil side of a person always be stronger?
  c If Dr Jekyll had not used all the impure salt, do you think he would have continued with his Jekyll and Hyde life?

Writing

39 Compare Dr Jekyll and Mr Hyde. How are they similar and different in appearance, character and behaviour?

40 Read the opening paragraph of the story again. Imagine you are sitting next to Mr Utterson at a dinner party. Write a short conversation between you and Mr Utterson.

41 Write a paragraph contrasting the street round the corner from Dr Jekyll's house and the Soho street where Mr Hyde lives.

42 You are Mr Hyde's housekeeper in Soho. Write a statement for the police, including everything you know about Mr Hyde and his visits to the house.

43 Write a story for a London newspaper with the headline 'Hyde Takes Own Life'. Give as many facts as you can and include interviews with the servants.

44 Imagine a person with a different kind of double life: happy and depressed; adventurous and shy; charming and cruel. Describe an event where they show both sides of their character.

45 Are there areas of scientific experimentation today that you are not comfortable with? Explain why (not).

Answers for the Activities in this book are available from the Pearson English Readers website. A free Activity Worksheet is also available from the website. Activity worksheets are part of the Pearson English Readers Teacher Support Programme, which also includes Progress tests and Graded Reader Guidelines. For more information, please visit: www.pearsonenglishreaders.com

WORD LIST

anxiety (n) a strong feeling of worry about something that may happen

approve (v) to believe that someone or something is acceptable

ash (n) the soft grey powder that is left after something has been burned

awkward (adj) embarrassed and shy

axe (n) a tool with a wooden handle and a metal blade, used for cutting wood

blackmail (n) the act of threatening to tell someone's secrets if they don't pay you money or do what you want

butler (n) the most important male servant in a big house

candle (n) a stick of wax that gives light when it burns

carriage (n) a vehicle pulled by horses

companion (n) someone who you spend a lot of time with

despair (n/v) a feeling of great happiness and no hope

distaste (n) a feeling of strong dislike

experiment (n) a scientific test to find out or prove something

fancy (n) a feeling that you like something; an idea that is unlikely

influence (n) the power to affect the way that someone behaves or thinks

locksmith (n) someone who makes and repairs locks

lung (n) one of two parts of your body that you use for breathing

mask (n) something that covers all or part of your face to protect or hide it

misery (n) a feeling of great unhappiness

muscle (n) one of the pieces of flesh that join your bones together and make your body move; if you are **muscular**, you have a lot of big muscles

neglect (n) the failure to look after someone or something

relief (n) the feeling that you have when you stop worrying about something; you are **relieved**

rusty (adj) covered with the red-brown substance that forms on wet metal

scorn (n/v) an opinion that someone or something is stupid or worthless

seal (n/v) a piece of wax, often with a personal or official stamp on it, that was used to close letters and documents in the past

sigh (v) to breathe out heavily because you are, for example, tired, bored or annoyed

suspicion (n) the feeling that someone has done something wrong or that something may be true

tempt (v) to make someone want to do or have something even if it is wrong

tremble (v) to shake because you are worried, afraid or excited

victim (n) a person who has been hurt or killed by someone or something

Better learning
comes from fun.

Pearson English **Readers**

There are plenty of Pearson English Readers to choose from - world classics, film and television adaptations, short stories, thrillers, modern-day crime and adventure, biographies, American classics, non-fiction, plays ... and more to come.

For a complete list of all Pearson English Readers titles, please contact your local Pearson Education office or visit the website.

pearsonenglishreaders.com

LONGMAN
Dictionaries

Express yourself with confidence

Longman has led the way in ELT dictionaries since 1935. We constantly talk to students and teachers around the world to find out what they need from a learners' dictionary.

Why choose a Longman dictionary?

EASY TO UNDERSTAND

Longman invented the Defining Vocabulary - 2000 of the most common words which are used to write the definitions in our dictionaries. So Longman definitions are always clear and easy to understand.

REAL, NATURAL ENGLISH

All Longman dictionaries contain natural examples taken from real-life that help explain the meaning of a word and show you how to use it in context.

AVOID COMMON MISTAKES

Longman dictionaries are written specially for learners, and we make sure that you get all the help you need to avoid common mistakes. We analyse typical learners' mistakes and include notes on how to avoid them.

DIGITAL INNOVATION

Longman dictionaries are also available online at:
www.longmandictionaries.com or **www.longmandictionariesusa.com**

These are premier dictionary websites that allow you to access the best of Longman Learners' dictionaries, whatever you do, wherever you are. They offer a wealth of additional resources for teachers and students in the Teacher's Corner and the Study Centre.

Notes:

Notes:

Notes:

_____

_____

_____

_____

_____

_____

_____

_____

_____

_____

_____

_____

_____

_____

_____

_____

_____